P9-CLA-523

How To Catch Pike & Muskie

NORTH AMERICAN FISHING CLUB

MINNETONKA, MINNESOTA

Dick Sternberg's pioneering research on the coldwater habits of northern pike has dramatically changed the way anglers fish for these top-rung predators.

How To Catch Pike & Muskie

Copyright © 2000 North American Fishing Club

All rights reserved. No part of this publication may be reproduced, stored in an electronic retrieval system or transmitted in any form or by any means (electronic, mechanical, photocopying, recording or otherwise) without the prior written permission of the copyright owner.

Mike Vail
Vice President,
Product & Business Development

Tom Carpenter
Director of Book Development

Dan Kennedy
Book Production Manager

Jenya Prosmitsky
Book Design & Production

Gina Germ
Photo Editor

Michele Teigen
Book Development Coordinator

Kay Thompson
Proofreading

Principle Photography
Bill Lindner Photography (Bill Lindner, Mike Hehner, Tom Heck, Pete Cozad, Jason Lund)

Additional Photography
Jan Eggers aka The Pike Ferret p. 18 both; Grand Rapids Herald Review/Cass County Museum 29; Dick Sternberg pp. 47(3), 95, 108, 129, 135, 136, 137, 138, 153; Dan Kennedy pp. 70(2), 71; Fishing Hot Spots Maps pp. 125, 147; Muskies Inc., International Office, 2301 7th Street North, Fargo, ND 58102, Telephone 701.239.9540, WEB www.muskieinc.org p. 153

Illustration
**Joe Tomelleri pp. 11(2), 13(2), 15 all
Maynard Reece p. 14 all
David Schelitzsche pp. 15(2), 98
Bill Reynolds pp. 25, 63, 111, 128 both, 137, 143, 145
Jenya Prosmitsky p. 79**

Special Thanks to:
**Marine Metal Products
Pure Fishing
St. Croix Rods**

9 8 7 6 5 4 3 2 1
ISBN 1-58159-079-2

North American Fishing Club
12301 Whitewater Drive
Minnetonka, MN 55343

CONTENTS

INTRODUCTION

Author Dick Sternberg is correct when he says pike and muskies "have inspired so many fanciful tales that it is difficult to separate fact from fiction."

Anglers have been led to believe that catching a muskie means thousands of casts and many days on the water, when in fact top anglers hit the water expecting to catch a muskie, or even several, every day. The key is targeting prime spots on good waters and using the right bait or lure. Want to catch muskies (notice the "S")? Start with a solid understanding of the fish, and other aspects of your search will fall into place.

Catching a truly large pike is often more challenging than sticking a big muskie. First, there just aren't that many big pike around. Second, big pike and small pike are two different animals, and most anglers look for locations and use techniques that target small fish. But there are tricks to the trade. You'll find them, outlined in clear and concise detail, in the pages that follow.

Sternberg knows muskie and pike. But more than that, he is a fishing expert. This former fisheries biologist applies science to fishing, combines the two better than anyone I know, and catches fish that others only dream about.

How To Catch Pike & Muskie is a must-read title for both beginning and serious pursuers of these top predators.

I've studied every word here—this book is a winner!

Steve Pennaz

Executive Director
North American Fishing Club

THE FISH

For consistent pike- and muskie-fishing success, you must learn to separate the myth and misinformation from the facts.

UNDERSTANDING NORTHERN PIKE, MUSKIES & HYBRIDS

Developing a solid understanding of pike and muskies is a challenge. Over the years, these top predators have inspired so many fanciful tales that it has become difficult to separate fact from fiction.

Pike and muskies are close-ly related; along with their smaller cousins the pickerel, they belong to the pike family (*Esocidae*) and are sometimes referred to as esocids. There are numerous similarities in the appearance and behavior of northern pike and muskies, but there are considerable dif-ferences as well. To be a successful pike and muskie angler, it's important to understand the unique characteristics of each species as well as those of the tiger muskie, a pike-muskie hybrid (p. 12).

How Pike and Muskie Differ

Besides the obvious physical differences (pp. 11-13), pike differ from muskies in many ways that have definite implications for anglers. Here are some of the most significant differences:

• Pike are native to northerly regions around the world. Muskies are native only to North America and their range does not extend as far north.

• Muskies grow faster and reach a larger size than North American pike. The North American record pike weighed only two-thirds as much as the record muskie. Eurasian pike, however, rival North American muskies in size.

• Although pike and muskies are both classified as cool-water fish, there is a definite difference in the water temperature they prefer, especially among the larger members of the species. Pike more than 30 inches long favor water temperatures from 50° to 55°F; big muskies prefer temperatures of 67 to 72.

• Pike feed actively throughout the year and are a popular target of ice fishermen. Muskies feed much more sporadically in winter and are seldom caught by ice anglers.

• Muskies feed much more selectively than pike, meaning that they're considerably more difficult to catch. A pike is likely to attack practically any kind of lure or bait that passes its way. But a muskie tends to examine your offering much more closely, often following it for a ways and then turning away at the last second.

• Pike spawn at cooler water temperatures than muskies, meaning that they hatch earlier in the spring. By the time muskies hatch, the young pike are big enough to eat them. This explains why most waters with both species hold considerably more pike than muskies.

The muskie's habit of following a bait all the way to the boat and then turning away at the last instant is a constant frustration for anglers.

NORTHERN PIKE BASICS

Northern pike have the ability to adapt to an extremely wide variety of habitat, explaining why they have a circumpolar distribution. In North America, they're found at latitudes from 40 to 70°N, which includes most of the northern U.S. and Canada. Some of the world's best trophy-pike waters are in Europe and Siberia.

Northern pike rate highly among anglers because of their cooperative nature. Even on cold-front days or under other adverse conditions that shut down most other game-fish, you can generally catch a few pike.

But their willingness to bite also causes problems for fish managers. In heavily fished waters, the pike are removed so quickly that they never have a chance to grow to a decent size. Consequently, anglers catch only "hammer-handles." This explains why the biggest pike are caught in remote areas of Canada, and in big lakes in which anglers focus primarily on other kinds of fish.

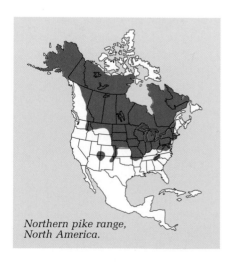

Northern pike range, North America.

***Northern Pike* (Esox lucius).** *Pike (top) have dark greenish sides with 7 to 9 rows of oval-shaped, cream-colored marks. They have a single dorsal fin located far back on the body. The fins usually have dark blotches and a reddish tinge. The underside of the jaw usually has 10 pores (above left) and the entire cheek and top of the gill cover are scaled (above right).* **World Record:** *55 pounds, 1 ounce; Lake of Grefeern, West Germany; October 16, 1986.*

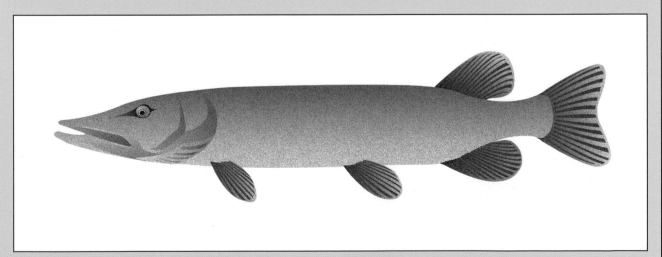

Silver Pike. *This is a mutant form of northern pike found occasionally throughout the pike's range. Silver pike have silvery, metallic-blue or greenish sides without the typical light, oval-shaped markings.*

MUSKIE BASICS

Although muskies have a much smaller range than northern pike, many anglers consider them the ultimate gamefish. Not only do muskies rank among the largest and hardest-fighting of all freshwater gamefish species, they are one of the most challenging to catch.

Muskies have much more selective feeding habits than pike, and their population density is never as high. This explains why they're sometimes called "the fish of 10,000 casts." But don't be intimidated by their reputation. Once you develop an understanding of muskie behavior and locational patterns, you won't have to wait nearly that long.

The appearance of muskies is much more variable than that of northern pike. While there is only one species of muskie, there are three distinct color phases (p. 14) as well as several intergrades between these color phases.

Tiger Muskie

These pike-muskie hybrids further complicate the muskie identification problem. Although tiger muskies occur naturally in some waters, the majority of them are stocked. In fact, tiger muskies have become so popular in some states that very few purebred muskies are being planted.

Produced by mixing northern pike sperm with muskie eggs, tiger muskies are popular among fish culturists because they're easier to raise than purebred muskies. Hybrids will take a wider variety of foods, and are more resistant to disease and thermal stress. They're a favorite of anglers because they're much easier to catch than purebred muskies. Although they don't grow quite as large, hybrids usually reach a considerably larger size than pike in the same waters.

Muskellunge range.

Muskellunge (Esox masquinongy). *Muskies (top) have dark spots or bars on light greenish to silvery sides. Or they may be unmarked. The tail has sharper lobes and smaller spots than that of a northern pike, or it may have no spots. The underside of a muskie's lower jaw has 12 to 18 pores (above left) and only the top half of a muskie's cheek and gill cover are scaled (above right).* **World Record:** *69 pounds, 11 ounces; Chippewa Flowage, Wisconsin; October 20, 1949.*

Tiger Muskie. *This is a cross between a muskie and a northern pike. It has light sides with dark, vertical bars, which are often broken into spots. The lobes of the tail are rounder than those of a true muskie.* **World Record:** *51 pounds, 3 ounces; Lac Vieux Desert, Wisconsin; July 16, 1919.*

Muskie Color Phases

Clear Muskie. *The sides are usually brownish or greenish, with no vertical bars or spots.*

Barred Muskie. *The light greenish to silvery sides have dark, wide vertical bars.*

Spotted Muskie. *The brownish to greenish sides have randomly-spaced rounded spots or blotches.*

How To Catch Pike & Muskie

Chain pickerel range.

Chain Pickerel* (Esox niger).** *These fish have a greenish to bronze background coloration with a dark chain-link pattern, explaining the name "chain pickerel." The entire cheek and gill cover are scaled and there are 8 pores on the underside of the lower jaw.* ***World Record: *9 pounds, 6 ounces; Guest Millpond, Georgia; February 17, 1961.*

Redfin pickerel range.

Redfin Pickerel* (Esox americanus americanus).** *The snout is shorter than that of a chain pickerel and the sides are light brownish to greenish with dark vertical bars. The pale areas between the bars are narrower than the bars themselves. There is a distinct dark bar below the eye that usually curves to the rear. The lower fins have a reddish hue.* ***World Record: *2 pounds, 4 ounces; Gall Berry Swamp, North Carolina; June 27, 1997.*

Grass pickerel range.

Grass Pickerel* (Esox americanus vermiculatus).** *This subspecies of the redfin pickerel resembles the redfin but is even smaller. The pale areas between the vertical bars are wider than the bars themselves and the dark bar below the eye is usually straight. The lower fins are greenish.* ***World Record: *1 pound; Dewart Lake, Indiana; June 9, 1990.*

FOOD HABITS

Most anglers regard pike and muskies as "eating machines," intent on attacking practically anything that will fit into their mouth. While it's true that they will eat prey of incredible size, they really eat no more than any other fish of comparable weight.

From the time they grow large enough to begin feeding, pike and muskies eat surprisingly large prey. In fact, they generally prefer one very large food item to several small ones. They tend to select foods from ¼ to ⅓ of their own length and, on occasion, will attack prey ½ their length.

Although they feed on plankton and invertebrates during their first weeks of life, pike and muskies soon start to focus almost entirely on smaller fish. But when the opportunity presents itself, they will take mice, frogs, salamanders, crayfish, leeches, snakes, ducklings, squirrels, muskrats and other small mammals.

Pike and muskies prefer long-bodied, soft-finned baitfish such as ciscoes, smelt or suckers. But they do not hesitate to eat deep-bodied, spiny-rayed fish like sunfish or crappies, even though fish of this type are more likely to lodge in their throat.

While many gamefish cruise about in search of food, pike and muskies are more likely to lie motionless, waiting for the prey to make a mistake and swim too close. As the prey approaches, they

Pike and muskies save energy by ambushing their prey.

curl their body into a snake-like "S" and then uncoil at lightning speed, striking the prey at speeds of nearly 30 mph. This explains why they are called "sprint predators."

Pike are primarily daytime feeders and seldom bite after dark. Muskies, however, will feed aggressively at night, especially in very clear lakes or in lakes where boat traffic is heavy during the day. Both species feed most heavily when skies are overcast. But in very muddy or discolored water, they're often more active in sunny weather.

Food-habit studies have shown that pike feed most heavily at a water temperature of about 65°F. Food con-

sumption drops greatly at temperatures above 75. Pike continue to feed at near-freezing temperatures in winter, but they consume only about 10 percent as much food as they do during the peak feeding period.

Muskie feeding peaks at a water temperature of about 70°F, gradually declines up to a summertime temperature of about 80 and then stops almost completely until the water starts to cool in fall. Muskies often go on a late-fall feeding binge, but the action grinds to a halt once the water temperature drops below 40. This explains why very few muskies are caught by ice fishermen.

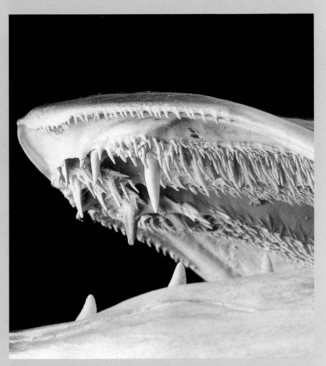

1 Pike and muskies grab a baitfish any way they can—by the head, by the tail or sideways (left). Recurved teeth on the roof of the mouth (right) prevent the prey from escaping and the long, sharp teeth along the edges of the jaw puncture the prey to kill it.

2 After the baitfish stops struggling, the pike or muskie loosens its grip and turns the prey to swallow it headfirst. This way, the dorsal fin of the prey folds back so it doesn't catch in the pike or muskie's throat.

3 If the prey is too large to swallow completely, a pike or muskie will swallow only as much as it can. The tail of the prey protrudes from the fish's mouth until they digest enough of the body to allow them to swallow a little more.

GROWTH

The growth rate of pike and muskies varies tremendously throughout their range depending primarily on the following:

• **Latitude.** Pike and muskies generally grow faster in the southern part of their range than in the northern part (opposite), because the southern part has a longer growing season.

But the faster growth rate in southern waters does not necessarily mean that the fish reach larger size. Pike, for instance, are usually smaller in the extreme southern part of their range because water temperatures there are too warm for optimal growth.

Another reason that pike and muskies are often smaller in southern waters is that they don't live as long. In frigid northern lakes, for example, both species have been known to live more than 25 years. In southern waters,

Northern pike found in Europe (above photos) and Asia are heavier-bodied than North American pike, and rival the muskie in size.

muskies seldom live more than 12 years and pike usually live less than half that long.

Even in waters at the same latitude, the growth rate of pike and muskies varies considerably. For instance, pike often grow faster in deep lakes than in shallow ones nearby, because the shallow lakes warm uniformly from top to bottom and exceed the pike's preferred feeding temperature.

• **Food Supply.** All other factors being equal, pike and muskies grow fastest in waters with an abundance of high-fat forage such as smelt, ciscoes or other salmonids, including stocked trout.

• **Stunting.** Muskies seldom reach a population density high enough to cause stunting, but pike commonly do. One of the biggest problems is fishing pressure; when too many of the big pike are removed, small pike dominate, often exhausting the food supply. Their growth rate slows dramatically, resulting in a population of "hammer-handles."

• **Genetics.** Biologist are finding that certain varieties of muskies grow considerably faster than others. For example, Wisconsin-strain muskies stocked in Minnesota waters grew considerably faster than two different Minnesota strains.

Although there is less genetic variability among northern pike, European and Asian pike usually weigh more than North American pike of the same length (see chart).

Typical Weight of European vs. North American Pike

Length (inches)	Weight (Pounds)	
	N. American Pike	European Pike
21	2.3	2.9
24	3.2	4.3
27	4.6	6.2
30	6.6	8.4
33	8.1	11.2
36	10.5	14.6
39	15.3	18.5
42	18.6	23.2
45	22.0	28.5

Growth of Pike and Muskies at Various Latitudes*

	Length (Inches) at Each Age							
Pike	1	3	5	7	9	11	13	15
Great Slave Lake, NWT (62°N)	4.2	8.6	13.2	17.5	21.3	24.7	28.6	33.5
Saskatchewan River , SK (54°N)	4.2	14.7	22.0	24.8	31.5	—	—	—
Lake Vermilion, MN (47°N)	7.6	16.8	22.5	29.0	34.6	38.9	—	—
Lake Mendota, WI (43°N)	11.4	26.9	33.7	37.9	—	—	—	—
Muskellunge								
Maskinonge Lake, ON (50°N)	—	22.0	27.2	27.7	30.1	34.5	—	40.0
Lac Court Orielles, WI (46°N)	8.6	20.5	27.2	31.6	36.4	—	—	—
Conneaut Lake, PA (42°N)	6.7	21.5	31.1	37.7	44.6	47.2	50.4	54.0
Pomme de Terre Lake, MO (38°N)	12.2	29.1	36.7	42.2	—	—	—	—

* Growth data for older fish not available in many waters in the southern part of range because the fish there have a shorter life span in the warmer water.

How Growth Rate Affects Body Shape

Fast-growing pike usually have deep, wide bodies and relatively small heads.

Slow-growing pike have skinny bodies, explaining why they're called hammerhandles. The head is usually large for the size of the body.

Pike and muskies rely mainly on eyesight to track their prey.

SENSES

Although there have been few conclusive scientific studies on the sensory capabilities of pike and muskies, anglers and researchers have formed some definite opinions based on years of observation.

• Both species are sight-oriented. Their large eyes, located toward the top of the head, are highly movable. A pike or muskie in an aquarium will immediately focus its eyes on a minnow dropped into the water and will intently track the minnow with its eyes until making the decision to strike.

The fact that muskies are seldom found in low-clarity waters suggests that they are even more sight-oriented than pike, which commonly thrive in murky lakes and rivers.

• Muskies have better night vision than pike. Night stalkers know that muskies can easily be caught at night, while pike seldom bite after dark.

• Both species have a strong lateral-line sense. Rows of pores along the midline of the body, on the head and beneath the jaw pick up any slight vibration in the water, including vibrations produced by swimming baitfish. Tiny hairs inside the pores transmit the vibrations to nerve endings, enabling the the fish to locate prey even in waters where it cannot see.

Tests conducted by German researchers in the early 1900s conclusively demonstrated the importance of the lateral-line sense. After severing the pikes' optic nerves, they found that the fish could still track and catch live baitfish, apparently by using the lateral-line sense.

• The sense of smell is of only minimal importance. In fact, researchers investigating the sense of smell in pike concluded that the fish do not respond to the smell of food at all. But anglers using dead smelt or other oily fish for pike bait know better. These smelly dead baitfish often work better than live ones.

Lures that Appeal to Esocid Senses

A flashy spoon appeals mainly to the sense of sight and is one of the most reliable clear-water pike producers.

The thumping blade of a bucktail or spinnerbait appeals strongly to both the sense of sight and the lateral-line sense, explaining why these lures work so well for pike and muskies.

Pores along the midline and on the head (inset) of pike and muskies are part of their lateral-line system, which is of primary importance in tracking prey.

Pike work their way up streams that are only a few inches deep to reach their spawning grounds.

SPAWNING HABITS

Pike and muskies are spring spawners, depositing their eggs in shallow portions of lakes and streams, usually in areas with an abundance of aquatic plants. All esocids are random spawners rather than nest builders and, once the eggs have been deposited, the parents abandon them and make no attempt to protect the young.

Although there are many similarities in the spawning habits of pike and muskies, there are some differences as well:

• Pike spawn earlier in the season than muskies. Even before ice-out on northern lakes, pike swim up small tributary streams to spawn in nearby marshes that are free of ice. They also spawn in shallow bays of lakes or in weedy river backwaters. Spawning usually takes place at water temperatures in the low 40s.

Muskies spawn anywhere from 2 to 5 weeks later than pike, generally at water temperatures in the upper 40s to upper 50s. They scatter their eggs in weedy bays or over main-lake weed flats.

but muskies (especially the large females) may not feed for several weeks.

• Muskies often spawn in deeper water than pike. Muskies generally deposit their eggs at depths of 2 to 6 feet; pike, 6 inches to 3 feet.

• The hatch rate of pike is greater than that of muskies. Pike eggs are adhesive, so they cling to the weeds. Muskie eggs are not adhesive, so many of them sink to the bottom and settle into the mud where they die from oxygen starvation. This partially explains why muskies are seldom as abundant as pike. The other reason is that young pike get a considerable head start in growth, so they are large enough to prey on newly hatched muskie fry.

Violent splashes in a shallow bay are a good indication of muskie spawning activity. Males thrash their tails wildly to scatter the eggs, often resulting in split fins and deep gashes on their tails.

To test the survival rates of pike and muskie fry, fisheries researchers stocked 25,000 of each into a small pond. After 1 month, they recovered 409 pike but only 4 muskies.

Typical Spawning Habitat

Muskies commonly spawn in weedy bays but they deposit their eggs in slightly deeper water than that used by pike.

Shallow marshes connected to lakes and rivers make ideal spawning areas for pike. In some cases, fisheries managers dam these marshes after spawning has been completed. This maintains the water level until the young are ready to leave.

It's important for pike and muskie anglers to understand the timing of these spawning cycles, because they have a dramatic effect on fishing. Males move onto the spawning areas several days before the females, and they usually remain for a week or two after spawning has been completed. Both species feed heavily prior to spawning, but they do not feed once spawning begins and are seldom caught. Pike resume feeding soon after spawning,

LORE, LEGEND & MYTHS

No other freshwater game-fish have inspired as many incredible stories—and generated as much misinformation—as the northern pike and muskie.

One such tall tale is the legend of the "Emperor's Pike," a behemoth pulled from a German lake in 1497. As the story goes, the pike was first caught in the year 1230 by Emperor Frederick II, who placed an engraved copper ring around its body and then released it. When the fish was caught for the second time 267 years later, it supposedly weighed 550 pounds and measured 19 feet in length. Years later, when

someone got around to examining the preserved carcass, they uncovered a hoax: The backbone consisted of vertebrae from several different pike.

Even Sir Isaac Walton couldn't resist telling a giant pike tale in his 1615 book, *The Compleat Angler*. It seems that the clerk of the local parish was doing some trolling when he hooked a monster pike estimated to weigh 170 pounds. In describing what happened next, Walton says, "... his bait was seized by this furious creature, which by a sudden jerk pulled him in, and doubtless would have

devoured him, had he not by wonderful agility and dextrous swimming escaped the dreadful jaws of this voracious animal."

Tales of encounters with giant pike and muskies are rampant even in modern times. A few decades ago, a giant pike seen from time to time on a northern Wisconsin lake was fondly referred to as "Jingle Bells"; it had broken so many lines that all the spoons hanging from its jaws jingled whenever it jumped.

There have been numerous reports (many legitimate) of muskies raising havoc with swimmers. In one Minnesota lake, a swimming beach

recently had to be closed for several days to get rid of a rogue muskie that had found its way inside a net intended to cordon off the swimming area; the fish had badly bitten a young boy, requiring many stiches.

Although lore and legend will always be an important part of pike and muskie fishing, they have helped create a belief that these fish are fierce super-predators, intent on devouring everything that swims in a given body of water. In an article that appeared in a 1956 edition of *Field & Stream* magazine, writer Harry Botsford says, "I have always believed that a bounty should be paid for big muskies. Often they kill for the sheer fun of it, and the destruction they can do in an hour can be appalling."

That attitude has led to an anti-pike and muskie sentiment among many anglers. They believe that walleyes, bass and other "more desirable" gamefish suffer when a lake has too many of these vicious predators.

Despite efforts on the part of conservation agencies, sportsmen's organizations and outdoor writers to dispel misconceptions about pike and muskies, many of the old myths still persist (next page). Muskie stocking programs, in particular, have faced staunch opposition in many areas as anglers have campaigned to prevent their introduction into new waters.

There's no doubt that muskies eat other gamefish. But in most waters there are too few muskies to comprise a serious threat.

5 Common Pike and Muskie Myths

#1-Pike lose their teeth in the summer and don't bite.

This common misconception stems from the fact that pike and muskies continually shed old teeth and grow new ones. An angler who has been experiencing poor summertime pike fishing finally catches a pike and notices that some of the teeth are missing. He assumes that the reason fishing has been so lousy is that the fish have "sore mouths."

It's true that pike fishing deteriorates in many waters during the summer months, but the decline is probably related to a glut of baitfish available or the fact that pike often move into deeper, cooler water as the summer progresses. The problem is: Most anglers just aren't fishing where the fish are.

#2-Pike are full of bones and not much good to eat.

There's no arguing the fact that northern pike have lots of "Y" bones, but these bones can easily be removed during the filleting process. In some waters, saving a few pike to eat is acceptable. Fish connoisseurs give pike a very high table-quality rating; they have firm, white, flaky meat with no "fishy" taste.

Although muskies are also good-eating, most conscientious anglers choose to release them. They're worth more in the water than on the dinner table.

#3-Muskies are "eating machines," consuming everything in sight—including my favorite gamefish.

The notion that muskies are super-predators is false. Like any other gamefish, they eat what they

Here's evidence that pike and muskies will attack other gamefish.

need to survive, but they aren't willy-nilly killers and they don't eat any more than other fish of the same size.

But that doesn't mean that they can't have an impact on your fishing success. In certain situations, a big muskie moves into a spot and drives out many of the smaller fish. An angler notices that the fish are gone and assumes that the muskie has eaten them.

#4-I heard that the conservation department just netted a world-record muskie in my favorite lake.

Rumors like this pop up every year, but very few—if any—are true. Those netted fish, like the ones caught by anglers, have a way of growing each time the story is told.

Over the years, there have been many stories of 100-pound-plus muskies taken by survey crews, but none of these reports has ever been confirmed.

The bottom line: Don't chase rumors of big muskies until you've

taken the time to research their validity from a reliable source.

#5-There's been a big muskie hanging around here for years, but nobody can catch it.

Many anglers believe that a big muskie will move into a particular spot and take up permanent residence, sometimes living there for years. While that is seldom the case, it may seem that way because certain spots consistently hold a big muskie.

As a rule, the biggest muskies tend to select the spots that offer the best cover and the most food. When someone catches a big muskie from a spot like this, another fish of about the same size often moves in to take its place.

Fishermen who consistently see a muskie in this type of spot assume that it's the same fish they've seen there in the past when, in fact, that fish may have died or been removed by an angler.

PIKE & MUSKIE CONSERVATION

Strong conservation measures are needed to manage practically any fish population, but they are especially important in pike and muskie management. Both species are extremely vulnerable to overfishing, for different reasons.

The pike's aggressive nature makes it possible for anglers to quickly remove the biggest fish, leaving large numbers of pike that are too small to interest fishermen. Muskies are much more difficult to catch, but their low population density means that few to no fish can be removed without endangering the fishery. This explains why many conservation agencies have adopted special fishing regulations, such as minimum size limits. Special regulations are almost universal for muskies and are becoming much more common for pike.

While there is little doubt that more stringent regulations will be needed to maintain pike and muskie populations in the future, a few

Catch-and-release fishing is a must for maintaining quality pike and muskie fishing.

states and provinces still allow the controversial practice of darkhouse spearing of northern pike through the ice. Decades ago, when pike were considered "snakes," trash fish not worthy of gamefish status, spearing was an acceptable method of harvest. But it's difficult to understand why any progressive conservation agency would allow pike spearing today.

Stocking of pike is seldom necessary, but muskies are

Serious Threats to Pike & Muskie Fishing

Few waters can stand up to catch-and-keep fishing of trophy pike and muskies. This historic photo shows a tremendous catch of trophy muskies taken during the infamous "muskie rampage" that occurred in the summer of 1955 on Minnesota's Leech Lake.

The outmoded practice of darkhouse spearing has destroyed the trophy potential of some of the north country's important pike waters.

commonly introduced as a "bonus" fish into waters where they are not native. But they should be stocked only in waters with few northern pike. Otherwise young-of-the-year pike eat most of the newly hatched muskies.

One of the most serious threats to pike and muskie populations is degradation or destruction of spawning habitat. A marsh area filled to build a new housing development, for example, may have been the prime pike spawning area for a nearby lake. Removal of aquatic vegetation by lakeshore property owners, or burgeoning roughfish populations, can also degrade spawning habitat.

When photographing a large pike or muskie that you want to release, be sure the person holding it supports it with both hands, one beneath the head and the other just behind the belly. If you hoist a heavy fish by the gills, you may tear the gill arch and kill the fish.

CATCH-AND-RELEASE

Thanks primarily to the strong educational efforts of private fishing organizations such as Muskies, Inc., catch-and-release has become the rule rather than the exception in muskie fishing, and that ethic is rapidly spreading among pike anglers.

But despite their good intentions, too many anglers do not know how to properly land and unhook these big fish so they can be successfully released. In one study on the success of catch-and-release muskie fishing, 40 percent of the muskies released did not survive, mainly because of lactic acid buildup in the blood.

One of the biggest mistakes is using tackle that is too

light. Light tackle may add to the sport but, by the time you wear the fish out enough to land it, the lactic acid level is off the chart and the fish cannot possibly recover. It may swim away but it will probably be dead the next day.

Another common mistake is hoisting the fish by the gills. If you're putting too much pressure on the gill arch and the fish starts flopping in your hand, the arch will probably tear and the fish may not recover.

However you choose to land the fish, try to get it back into the water as soon as possible. Or, better yet, don't take it out of the water: Release it at boatside. If you bring the fish into the boat and let it flop around for a couple minutes while you try to untangle

it from the net and remove the hooks, your chances for a successful release are minimal.

The latest catch-and-release fad is "plunging," dropping the fish nose-first from several feet above the surface to help it get down into the "cooler" water. The problem is, if the fish doesn't come around right away, it may float back up to the surface where it will have trouble righting itself. There, it could be attacked by gulls or hit by another boat.

Getting the fish into water a degree or two cooler will not help it recover. It's much better to hold the fish upright in the traditional manner (opposite) until it is revived.

Tips for a Successful Release

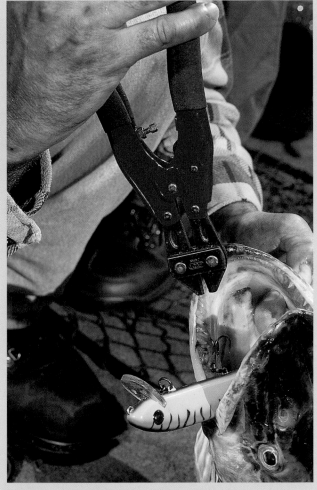

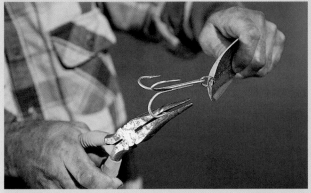

Land the fish with a cradle or a large net with plastic-coated mesh (p. 70). When you close up a cradle, it surrounds the fish's entire body so it cannot flop out of the net and injure itself. Leading a big fish into a cradle can be tricky, but some models have a V-shaped opening to make the job easier.

Flatten your hook barbs with a pair of pliers or file them off completely. You can remove barbless hooks in seconds and you'll seldom lose a fish, assuming you keep your line tight.

Carry a pair of sidecutters to clip off deeply embedded hooks. Dislodging the hooks takes too much time and the fish may not survive. Just slip new hooks onto the split rings and you'll be fishing again in seconds!

Revive the fish by gently rocking it in the water with one hand holding the tail and the other supporting the head. Hold the fish upright and try to keep water moving through its gills. When the fish can stay upright and swim on its own, it can safely be released.

THE WATERS

*T*here are
a lot of
similarities—
and a lot of
differences—in
the habitat
preferences of
pike and muskies.

PIKE & MUSKIE HABITAT

Describing what makes good pike habitat is difficult, because pike are one of the most adaptable species of freshwater fish. They're found at northerly latitudes around the globe, and they live in still waters ranging from warm ponds to frigid lakes and moving waters including everything from small trout streams to the largest warmwater rivers.

Muskies are far less versatile. Not only are their habitat requirements more specific, they are far less prolific and less competitive. In waters that hold both pike and muskies, for example, pike usually gain the upper hand.

Here are the major components of good pike and muskie habitat:

Water Temperature

While muskies and pike are both considered coolwater fish, the water temperatures they prefer are considerably different. Adult pike (over 30 inches long) favor a water temperature of 50° to 55°F; muskies prefer water from the mid 60s to low 70s, about the same as smaller pike.

Pike can tolerate a much wider temperature range than muskies. They're commonly found in lakes of the far North where the water temperature barely edges into the low 50s in summer, but they also live in lakes with summertime temperatures in the low 80s.

Muskies can withstand slightly warmer summertime water temperatures (around 85°F) but are rarely found in waters where the summertime temperature is less than 68. This explains why they inhabit a latitude range of 36 to 51°N, compared to a range of 40 to 70°N for pike.

Clarity

Pike inhabit some of the clearest waters in North America, but they're also found in muddy rivers and other low-clarity waters.

Muskies, on the other hand, prefer clear water and are seldom found in waters that stay permanently muddy or murky.

Oxygen

The reason pike can survive in shallow, fertile lakes is that they're very tolerant of the low oxygen levels found in these waters in severe winters, when heavy snow cover prevents sunlight from penetrating the ice. It's not unusual for pike to survive at oxygen levels as low as 1 part per million.

Muskies require considerably more oxygen in winter (about 2 ppm), so they are seldom found in shallow, fertile lakes.

Cover

Most anglers believe that heavy cover is a must for pike and muskies, but that is not necessarily the case. It's true that both species are commonly found in weedy cover, especially in broad-leaved weeds like cabbage, but they do not hesitate to leave this cover to find food or comfortable water temperatures.

In summer, for instance, muskies in deep, cold lakes often roam open water to feed on schools of suspended baitfish such as smelt or ciscoes. And pike descend into depths where there is no weed growth to find the cool water that they need during the hot summer months.

Home Range

With the exception of spawning migration, a muskie spends its entire life in a relatively small area, sometimes only a few hundred acres. But a pike roams more widely, frequently covering thousands of acres in large bodies of water.

The implications for anglers are obvious: When you see a muskie in a particular spot, there's a chance it will still be there the next time you return. The odds of a pike remaining in the same location are slim.

Current

Although pike and muskies are commonly found in rivers, neither species will tolerate much current. They prefer rivers with a gradient (drop) of less than 10 feet per mile. They may be found in rivers with faster current, however, if there are enough slow-moving backwater areas.

Pike can tolerate a wide range of environmental conditions, including murky or muddy water like this with a visibility of only a few inches.

NATURAL LAKES

North America is blessed with an abundance of pike water. A recent continent-wide inventory of esocid habitat revealed that there are about 266,000 square miles of water containing northern pike, 98 percent of which consists of natural lakes.

By comparison, muskie water is scarce. The inventory identified 4,870 square miles of water containing muskies, 72 percent of which consists of natural lakes.

On the following pages, we'll show you where to find pike and muskies in each major type of natural lake.

EUTROPHIC LAKES

Pike and muskies that swim in these shallow, fertile waters have a reputation as being to tough to catch, and for good reason: These lakes have tremendous crops of baitfish, so the fish are extremely well fed.

Another problem: Because of their high fertility, eutrophic lakes may have tremendous algal blooms which cloud the water in summer and make it difficult for the fish to see a lure or bait.

The high fertility level also means that the depths are probably devoid of oxygen

Pike and Muskie Locations in Eutrophic Lakes During...

Weedy hump.

Early Spring through Spawning
- Marshes connected to the main lake (pike).
- Shallow, weedy bays (pike and muskie).

Shallow, weedy bay.

Post-Spawn
- Weedlines and weedy humps and points, particularly those near spawning bays.
- Shallow gravel or rock bars.

Summer and Early Fall
- Beds of lily pads or other floating-leaved vegetation that keeps the water slightly cooler.

- Bars, points and flats with a healthy growth of submerged weeds, particularly cabbage.
- Edges of deep bulrush beds.
- Weedy saddles connecting two islands or a point and an island.
- Around coldwater inlets flowing into bays or boat harbors (pike).

Edge of deep bulrush bed.

Late Fall and Winter
- Deep, rocky humps.
- Deep holes surrounded by shallow water (in lakes that do not have low oxygen levels).

during the summer months, so savvy anglers know that the fish will be confined to the shallows. And the low water clarity means that weeds will not grow in deep water—more reason for the fish to stay shallow.

Pike and muskie fishing in these lakes is usually best in spring, before the young baitfish hatch, and in fall, when predation has thinned out the current year's baitfish. The water clarity is greater in spring and fall as well.

MESOTROPHIC LAKES

These moderately fertile lakes have good populations of baitfish, but not the forage glut common to so many eutrophic lakes. This means that pike and muskies have plenty to eat, yet they are generally more willing to bite than they are in most eutrophic lakes.

The water clarity in "meso" lakes is moderate as well, meaning that there is enough light penetration to allow good weed growth and the fish have no trouble seeing baits and lures.

Although some meso lakes have a shortage of oxygen in the depths during the summer months, pike and muskies usually inhabit a wider range of depths than they do in eutrophic lakes. At a minimum, they'll swim into the thermocline, which reaches depths of 25 or 30 feet in these waters.

After the fall turnover, when oxygen is restored to all depths, you may find pike and muskies in water as deep as 50 feet.

Yellow perch are usually the primary forage in shallow to mid-depth meso lakes. But in deep ones, pike and muskies often feed heavily on ciscoes. In summer, they follow cisco schools suspended in open water; this makes for tough fishing. In late fall, however, the ciscoes move up onto shallow, rocky reefs and shoal areas, and the pike are muskies are close behind.

Pike and Muskie Locations in Mesotrophic Lakes During...

Early Spring through Spawning
- Marshes connected to the main lake (pike).
- Shallow, weedy bays, especially those fed by a creek (pike and muskie).
- Shallow weed flats in the middle of large bays (muskies).

Shallow weed flat.

Shallow, weedy bay fed by a creek.

Post-Spawn
- Gravel bars and points just outside of spawning bays.
- Shoreline breaks in the vicinity of spawning bays.
- Shallow weed flats in the vicinity of spawning bays.

Summer and Early Fall
- Weedy points with an extended lip that slopes sharply into deep water.
- Edges of deep bulrush beds.
- Deep cabbage humps in the main lake.
- Weedy saddles between two islands or an island and a point.
- Suspended over open water in deep lakes with ciscoes or smelt.

- Mouths of good-sized inlet streams.
- Around coldwater inlets flowing into bays or boat harbors (pike).
- Rocky reefs below the thermocline (pike).
- Shallow, rocky reefs (muskie).
- Shallow, weedy bays (smaller pike).

Late Fall
- Shallow, gravelly reefs and shoal areas where ciscoes spawn when water temperatures reach the mid 40s.
- Deep holes where panfish congregate before freeze-up.
- Deep, rocky reefs.
- Sharp-sloping rocky points and humps.

Edge of deep bulrush bed.

Shallow, gravelly reef.

OLIGOTROPHIC LAKES

Although oligotrophic lakes have cold water and low fertility levels, some of these waters are top trophy pike and muskie producers.

Many "oli" lakes are in remote areas, so they see less fishing pressure than other kinds of natural lakes. But when these lakes become popular, the big fish are quickly removed.

One reason these waters produce so many trophies is that the fish utilize such a wide range of depths, making it difficult for anglers to find consistent locational patterns. With high oxygen levels at all depths, pike and muskies are caught on shallow reefs, in deep holes or anywhere in between. And they often pursue schools of suspended ciscoes in open water, just as they do in deep meso lakes.

In the far North, however, many lakes are so cold that pike stay in the shallow bays all summer, so anglers know exactly where to find them. These lakes are especially vulnerable to overfishing.

Because most of these lakes have rocky basins with steep-sloping shorelines, weed growth is relatively scarce. If

you do find a good weedbed, however, chances are it will hold fish.

Anglers should remember that pike and muskies grow very slowly in oligotrophic lakes, so catch-and-release fishing is of utmost importance. When it takes 20 years or more to grow a trophy-size fish, it's easy to understand why fishing quality would suffer if anglers kept big fish.

Pike and Muskie Locations in Oligotrophic Lakes During...

Early Spring through Spawning
• Mud-bottomed bays, particularly those with some weed growth.
• Shallow connecting lakes and marshes (pike).

Shallow, weedy bay.

Post-Spawn
• Shallow, weedy or rocky flats near spawning bays or inlets from connecting lakes.
• Channels between spawning bays and the main lake.
• Mouths of good-sized inlet streams.

Weedy main-lake hump.

Summer and Early Fall
• Narrows between two islands or an island and the main shoreline.
• Island clusters surrounded by deep water.

• Mouths of good-sized inlet streams.
• Sandy, weedy bays.
• Sandy, weedy humps.
• Rocky reefs.
• Main-lake points with an extended weedy lip.

Sandy, weedy bay.

Late Fall
• Shallow, gravelly reefs and shoal areas where ciscoes spawn when water temperatures reach the mid 40s.
• Deep, rocky reefs.
• Sharp-sloping rocky points and humps.
• Mouths of good-sized inlet streams.

Narrows between islands.

MAN-MADE LAKES

Although man-made lakes make up only 1.2 percent of the total pike water and 12.4 percent of the muskie water in North America, they have a history of producing some of the biggest fish. The record North American pike (46 pounds, 2 ounces) was caught in Sacandaga Reservoir, a 22,000-acre mid-depth reservoir in eastern New York, in 1940, and the world-record muskie (69 pounds, 11 ounces), was taken in the Chippewa Flowage, a shallow 15,300-acre reservoir in northern Wisconsin, in 1949.

SHALLOW RESERVOIRS

This category includes any type of man-made lake on relatively flat terrain. In the North, these waters are often called "flowages." Most of these lakes look much like any other shallow lake, but they usually have standing timber along the shoreline that was inundated when the dam was built.

Shallow reservoirs have warm, fertile water, usually of low clarity. Weed growth is minimal because of the limited light penetration and, in

Pike and Muskie Locations in Shallow Reservoirs During...

Early Spring through Spawning
- Marshy sections of the river above the reservoir.
- Marshy bays connected to the river above the reservoir.
- Main-lake bays with weedy or woody cover.

Main-lake bay.

Post-Spawn
- Shallow timbered humps near spawning bays.
- Points or flats with weedy or woody cover in the vicinity of spawning bays.
- Shallow gravel or rock bars near the mouth of the main river or just outside a spawning bay.

Summer and Early Fall
- Timbered flats or humps near the old river channel.
- Around coldwater inlets flowing into bays or boat harbors (pike).
- Around any significant beds of emergent or submerged weeds.
- Main-lake points near the old river channel.
- Man-made "cribs," brush piles or other types of fish attractors.

Timbered hump.

Late Fall
- Points that slope sharply into deep water.
- Deep, rocky humps.
- Deepest holes.

Flats near the old river channel.

some cases, high roughfish populations.

Pike and muskies may or may not be restricted to shallow water during the summer months, depending on the size of the stream feeding the lake. If the flow is only a trickle, the depths may be devoid of oxygen in summer (and in winter), meaning that the fish will be found at depths of 20 feet or less. In lakes fed by a good-sized stream, however, the fish can go much deeper.

The Waters

MID-DEPTH RESERVOIRS

This broad category of man-made lakes includes waters in hilly terrain, such as hill-land reservoirs in the southern and eastern states (muskies only), and impoundments on mainstem rivers such as the Missouri River reservoirs in the Dakotas (pike only). Although pike and muskies are native to some of these waters, the majority must be stocked.

Yearly water level fluctuations in many of these lakes are significant, limiting weed growth, so the fish rely mainly on woody or rocky cover. These fluctuations also limit spawning success, explaining the need for an ongoing stocking program.

Because of the fluctuating water levels, locational patterns are highly variable. A spot that held fish in late spring or early summer, for instance, may be high and dry by fall, so pike and muskies are forced to find new hangouts.

Adding to the difficulty of locating fish is the fact that many of these lakes have suspended forage, such as shad or smelt. Pike and muskies spend more of their time feeding in open water than they would in lakes where the primary forage is bottom-dwelling fish such as yellow perch.

Pike and Muskie Locations in Mid-Depth Reservoirs During...

Early Spring through Spawning

- Shallow creek arms, particularly those with an active feeder stream.
- Secondary creek arms off deeper arms.
- Shallow coves in the main lake or in large creek arms.
- Marshes connected to the main river channel above the reservoir (pike).

Main-lake rocky point.

Shallow cove.

Post-Spawn

- Gradually sloping points at the mouths of creek arms.
- Shallow timbered flats near the mouths of creek arms.
- Shorelines of deeper creek arms, particularly those with woody or rocky cover.

- Shallow main-lake gravel or rock bars, particularly those close to shore in the upper part of the lake.

Summer and Early Fall

- Main-lake rocky points, especially those close to the old river channel.
- Deep creek arms near the old river channel.
- The old river channel itself, especially in low-water periods.

- Suspended over deep water (in lakes with suspended forage).
- Around coldwater feeders flowing into deep creek arms (pike).
- Rocky or gravelly humps near the old river channel.
- Man-made fish attractors.
- Around emergent or submerged weedy cover.

Late Fall

- Tailwaters of upstream dams.
- Steep-sloping rocky points near the old river channel.
- Deep sections of the old river channel or deep creek channels.
- Deep, rocky reefs.

Shallow timbered flat.

Tailwater of an upstream dam.

DEEP RESERVOIRS

These man-made lakes have steep-sloping shorelines and a lot of deep, cold water in the depths. Examples of lakes in this category include Canadian shield reservoirs in Ontario and highland reservoirs in mountainous areas of the Southeast.

Canadian shield reservoirs differ from highland reservoirs in that their water levels are much more stable. Highland reservoirs are often drawn down in fall to make room for spring runoff, and their water levels may drop 50 feet or more. In most Canadian shield reservoirs, yellow perch and ciscoes are the main forage, and pike are more numerous than muskies. Shad are the primary forage in most highland reservoirs; muskies are native to some of these waters, but pike are rarely present.

Although both types of lakes have very clear water, only shield lakes have any significant amount of weedy cover. The fluctuating water in most highland reservoirs means that there is practically no weed growth.

Because these lakes have so much deep, cold, infertile water, pike and muskies are seldom numerous. But they grow to astounding size. Lac Suel Reservoir in Ontario, for instance, has long been recognized as one of North America's premier trophy muskie waters, producing several 50-pound-plus fish each year.

Pike and Muskie Locations in Deep Reservoirs During...

Early Spring through Spawning
- Shallow creek arms with active feeder streams.
- Secondary creek arms off deeper arms.
- Shallow coves in the main lake or in large creek arms.
- Weedy bays.
- Shallow connecting lakes and marshes (pike).

Shallow cove.

Post-Spawn
- Shallow, weedy or rocky flats near spawning bays or inlets from connecting lakes.
- Channels between spawning bays and the main lake.
- Mouths of good-sized inlet streams.
- Weedlines and weedy humps

and points, particularly those near spawning bays.
- Shallow gravel or rock bars.

Summer and Early Fall
- Narrows between two islands or an island and the main shoreline.
- Island clusters surrounded by deep water.
- Mouths of good-sized inlet streams.
- Sandy, weedy bays.
- Sandy, weedy humps.
- Rocky reefs.
- Main-lake points with an extended weedy lip.
- Main-lake rocky points close to the old river channel.
- Suspended over deep water (in lakes with suspended forage).
- Man-made fish attractors.
- Around emergent or submerged weedy cover.

Main-lake point.

Late Fall and Winter
- Shallow, gravelly reefs and shoal areas where ciscoes spawn when water temperatures reach the mid 40s.
- Deep, rocky reefs.
- Sharp-sloping rocky points and humps.
- Mouths of good-sized inlet streams.
- Tailwaters of upstream dams.

Shallow, weedy or rocky flats.

Rocky point.

RIVERS

Even though rivers and streams make up only 1.2 percent of North America's total pike water and 15.4 percent of the muskie water, they offer exceptional fishing in certain regions. For example, Canada's biggest muskie (a 65 pounder) was caught in the Moon River, a tributary to Lake Huron's Georgian Bay, in 1988. Quebec's Ottawa River produced the current catch-and-release record muskie, a 62-incher, in 1997. And the Northwest Territory's Mackenzie River has long been ranked among the top trophy pike waters in the world.

As a rule, muskies are better suited to life in rivers than pike. Because rivers do not stratify into temperature layers, pike cannot find the cool water they need during the summer, except in the northern states and Canada or in rivers with an ample flow of spring water.

Pike can survive in most any cool, unpolluted river that maintains a decent summertime flow and has enough slackwater area for the fish to escape the current. Muskies

Pike and Muskie Locations in Mid-Size Rivers During...

Early Spring through Spawning
- Sloughs connected to the river by high water in spring.
- Oxbow lakes still connected to the main river channel.

Slough connected to the river.

Post-Spawn through Early Fall
- Eddies in tailwater areas.
- Deep pools, especially those with light current and fallen trees or boulders for cover.
- Oxbow lakes still connected to the main river channel.

- Large eddies below points, sharp bends, islands, boulders, logjams or any other objects that break the current.
- Deep pools below rapids.
- Mouths of coldwater feeders (pike in summer and early fall).

Late Fall and Low-Water Periods
- The deepest holes in the river channel.
- Deep impounded areas above dams.

Deep hole in river channel.

Deep pool below rapids.

will put up with warmer water and more current, but they'll seldom tolerate water that stays muddy throughout the year.

SMALL TO MID-SIZE RIVERS

Pike and muskies abound in small to mid-size rivers, although these waters do not have the diversity of habitat and thus the trophy potential of big rivers.

An inventory of North American esocid habitat revealed that 80 percent of all pike rivers are less than 100 meters wide and 35 percent are less than 25 meters wide.

Small to mid-size rivers are even better suited to muskies, with 88 percent of all muskie rivers less than 100 meters wide and 44 percent less than 25 meters wide.

BIG RIVERS

A large river system has a network of backwaters, side channels and tributary streams that provides the habitat diversity that pike and muskies require. Besides good spawning areas and numerous cover options, these waters have a diversity of other fish species that provide a virtually inexhaustible supply of food.

Big rivers are top producers of trophy-caliber muskies. But unless they have a good supply of cool water in summer, they rarely produce truly large northern pike.

Where you find pike and muskies in big rivers depends mainly on water level and clarity. High water pushes the fish into flooded backwater areas or into tributaries with slower current. Low water keeps them in the main channel or in deep holes in backwater lakes. During low-water periods in the heat of summer, pike concentrate around around any pockets of cool water.

In rivers with relatively clear water, it's not unusual to find pike and muskies at depths of 30 to 40 feet. But in murky rivers, they're rarely deeper than 15 feet.

One reason big rivers produce so many quality pike and muskies is that they're so difficult to fish, especially for anglers not accustomed to dealing with moving water. Not only do changing water levels keep pike and muskies on the move, the fish scatter into backwaters and other flooded areas far from the main river channel during high-water periods.

Pike and Muskie Locations in Big Rivers During...

Early Spring through Spawning
- Backwater lakes, especially those with plenty of aquatic vegetation.
- Sloughs connected to the river by high water in spring.
- Oxbow lakes still connected to the main river channel.

- Deep backwaters with abundant weed growth.
- Weedy side channels connecting the main channel with a backwater lake.
- Weedy wing dams.
- Mouths of coldwater feeders (pike in summer and early fall).

Large eddy.

- Around springs flowing into marinas, bays or other protected areas (pike in summer and early fall).

Late Fall
- Weedy backwater lakes where panfish concentrate.
- Deep oxbows.
- Around warmwater discharges from power plants.
- Around spring holes where the water stays a little warmer than the main river.

Mouth of coldwater feeder.

Post-Spawn through Early Fall
- Eddies in tailwater areas.
- Oxbow lakes still connected to the main river channel.
- Large eddies below points, sharp bends, islands, gravel bars, boulders or any other objects that break the current.

Weedy backwater lake.

Side channel.

THE GEAR

If you have a weak spot in your equipment, these powerful fighters will help you find it.

How To Catch Pike & Muskie

RODS & REELS

Some serious pike and muskie anglers carry half a dozen different rod and reel combos for different fishing applications. But you really don't need that many outfits to catch fish. Most anglers can easily get by with 2 or 3 of the oufits described below:

All-Purpose Outfit

A medium-heavy to heavy-power graphite flippin' stick paired with a sturdy, high-speed baitcasting reel spooled with superline, Dacron or mono is a good all-around outfit for most types of pike and muskie fishing. It can be used for most live-bait presentations and will also handle the majority of artificials, with the exception of jerkbaits and lightweight lures such as small jigs and balsa minnowbaits.

Flippin' sticks, which are 7 to 7½ feet in length with an extra-long handle, are ideal for casting. Not only do these long rods give you more distance, they improve your accuracy as well.

Long rods have several other advantages:
• They enable you to steer your lure through "alleys" in the weeds.
• They make it possible to change directions quickly to trigger strikes.
• They allow you to make larger, smoother, deeper "figure 8s" (p. 77), increasing the chances that followers will grab your lure.
• They give you more hook-setting power and better control of hooked fish.
• They act as a shock absorber to minimize the chances of break-offs from sudden runs or head shakes.

All-purpose pike/muskie outfit.

Jerkbait outfit.

Jerkbait Outfit

A short, stiff baitcasting outfit is a must for jerkbait fishing. These lures are usually retrieved with downward strokes, so a rod that is too long will hit the water and interfere with your rhythm. For best results, your rod tip should fall just short of the water when you retrieve from your normal position. For the average angler, the right length is about 6 feet.

Stiffness is equally important; when a pike or muskie bites into a big wooden jerkbait, it takes a powerful rod and low-stretch line (Dacron or superline) to break the fish's hold on the lure enough to sink the hooks. Many anglers use "broomstick" rods for jerkbait fishing, but it pays to have a rod with a little "give" at the tip; otherwise the hooks may tear out when a big pike or muskie thrashes its head.

Spinning Outfit

Some pike and muskie anglers carry a 6- to 7-foot, medium-heavy power spinning outfit for casting light lures. Balsa minnowbaits, for example, would be difficult to cast with a heavy baitcasting outfit, but long casts are no problem with spinning gear and light mono or superline.

Spinning outfit.

How To Catch Pike & Muskie

Trolling Outfit

The all-purpose outfit mentioned earlier is adequate for most trolling presentations, with the exception of downrigger fishing and wire-line trolling. For downrigger fishing, use a slow-action, 8- to 8½-foot rod and a large-capacity, level-wind trolling reel. The long, soft rod can be doubled over in the rod

Trolling outfit.

holder; this way, it will take up some of the slack when it straightens out on a strike. The extra flex also cushions the shock from a powerful run.

Trolling outfit with wire line and roller guide.

What to Look for in a Baitcasting Reel

You can fish for pike and muskies with the same baitcasting reel you use for bass, but if there's a chance of catching trophy-sized fish, you'll need a larger, sturdier model. Here's what to look for:

• **A strong frame.** A reel with a plastic, graphite or flimsy metal frame will simply not stand up to as much hard use as one with a sturdy aluminum frame. The toughest models are machined from a solid aluminum blank, rather than stamped from thin sheet aluminum.

• **A wide spool.** A wide-spool reel not only holds plenty of heavy line, it casts much better than a narrow-spool reel. Because the line level does not fall as low on a long cast, the spool does not have to turn as fast. A low line level also reduces your retrieve speed.

• A smooth, steady drag. Most baitcasters used by pike/muskie anglers have star drags, but those on inexpensive models often have an "all-or-nothing" tension setting. Either the drag slips too much or not at all; it's difficult to adjust it properly. On top-shelf reels, the drag slips smoothly over a wide range of tension settings.

• **A high-gear ratio.** A high-speed reel is the best choice for casting most types of artificials. Select a reel with a gear ratio of at least 4.5:1. Slower reels will wear you out after a few hour of fishing and you'll waste too much time reeling in at the end of each cast.

• **A long handle.** The extra leverage provided by a long handle enables you to crank in hard-pulling lures with little effort, even on reels with a high gear ratio.

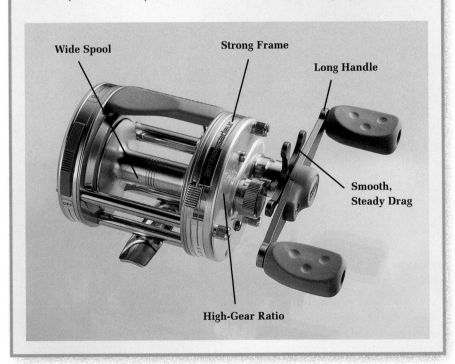

Although trolling with wire line has slipped in popularity since the introduction of the various superlines, some anglers maintain it's still the best way to troll for deepwater pike and muskies. But wire line will quickly groove an ordinary rod tip, so it's important to use a rod with a roller guide on the tip.

FISHING LINE

With line manufacturers introducing "revolutionary" new products every few months, it's no wonder that anglers get confused when it comes to selecting the right line for a certain fishing application.

The tendency is to buy every new product that comes out and spool it onto your favorite fishing outfit. But that can be a big mistake—the line may be ideal for one fishing purpose but disastrous for another. Here are some guidelines for helping you decide what kind of line to use for what kind of fishing:

Superline

These super-strong, no-stretch lines are exactly what you need for many kinds of pike and muskie fishing.

Because of their small diameter and limpness, they cast extremely well. The small diameter also means less water resistance, a big advantage in getting your lures to run deeper. And with virtually no stretch, superlines give you a powerful hookset.

But in some situations, the lack of stretch can be a disadvantage. For example, when you're retrieving a crankbait and you feel a slight tick, the tendency is to set the hook. In doing so, however, you may pull the lure away from the fish. With mono, there would be enough stretch to allow the fish to take the bait deep enough to get a solid hookset.

The lack of stretch can cause other problems as well: Lures may snap off on the cast, and you could break the line (or the rod) when setting the hook on a big fish or jerking on a snag.

Dacron

With the advent of superline, Dacron is not as popular as it once was, but it is still used by many pike and muskie anglers. Although its strength for the diameter is considerably less than superline, it has a little stretch so you're less likely to snap off lures or break lines or rods.

Monofilament

Because of its low visibility, mono is still an excellent choice in very clear water. Although pike and muskies are not as spooky as bass or walleyes, there are times (usually on calm, clear days) when they spot Dacron or superline and refuse to strike.

Because the fish tend to take a lure deeper with mono, it can improve your hooking percentage when they are striking short. Live-bait fishermen also rely heavily on mono; the extra stretch means that the fish feel less resistance when they pick up the bait, so they're less likely to drop it.

Anglers can select from dozens of different kinds of mono, but the main consideration is hardness. For optimal casting performance, choose a soft-finish, limp mono. For fishing in rocks or other cover that could fray your line, select a hard-finish, abrasion-resistant mono.

Fluorocarbon

The big advantage to fluorocarbon lines is that they're nearly invisible in the water. But early fluorocarbons were very stiff and very expensive, so they were used primarily to make leaders. Improved technology, however, has reduced the stiffness and lowered the price, so fishermen are now using them as a substitute for mono.

Wire Lines

Some trollers still swear by single-strand, stainless-steel wire line because it gets down even faster than superline. But wire line presents some unique problems: Besides grooving your rod tip, it tends to kink and requires special knots or connection methods (p. 61).

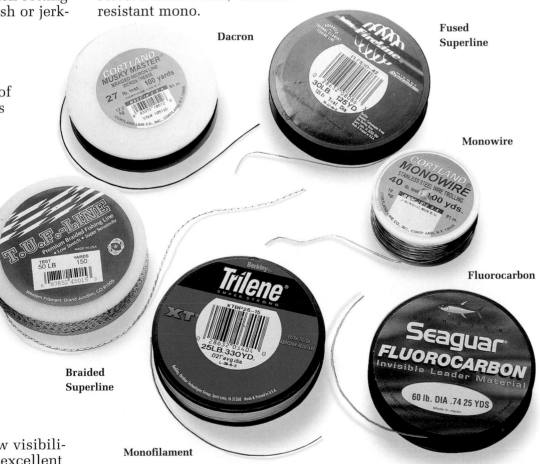

Dacron

Fused Superline

Monowire

Fluorocarbon

Braided Superline

Monofilament

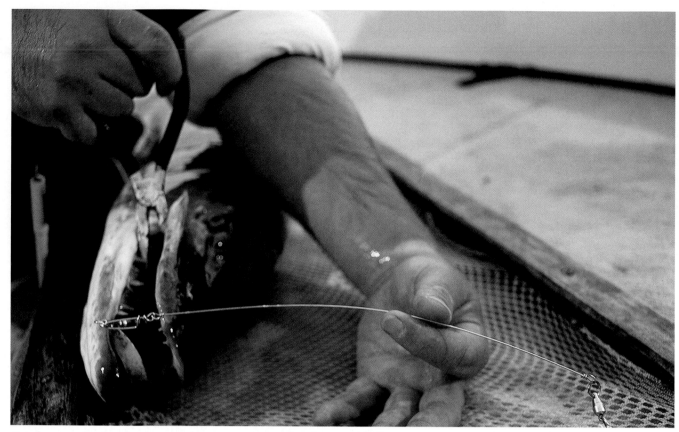

It takes a wire leader to stand up to an esocid's sharp-edged teeth.

LEADERS

A wire leader is a must in pike and muskie fishing. The fish have razor-sharp edges on their teeth that can easily sever practically any kind of fishing line, including superline.

A stiff wire leader is the best choice for lures that pull straight through the water, like bucktails and spinnerbaits. This type of leader won't kink so it will last indefinitely.

But a stiff, heavy leader would restrict the action of lures that wobble or vibrate, such as crankbaits, minnowbaits and rattlebaits. For these baits, you'll need a flexible braided-wire leader.

The problem with most braided leaders is that they won't stand much abuse. They kink easily when raked by the fish's sharp teeth, and they're impossible to straighten. A titanium leader solves the problem; it's very flexible but impossible to kink.

Whatever leader you select, be sure that it has sturdy swivels and clips. The powerful head thrashes of a big pike or muskie can easily open a cheap clip or break a light barrel swivel in half.

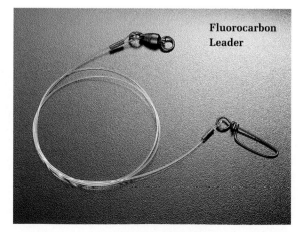

Fluorocarbon Leader

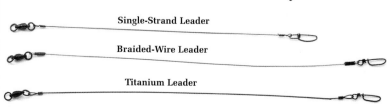

Single-Strand Leader

Braided-Wire Leader

Titanium Leader

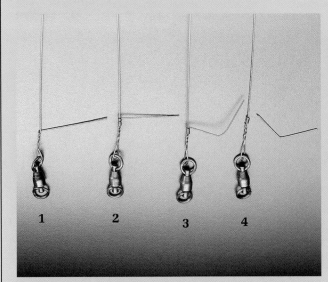

Single-Strand Wire Leader. *Attach a sturdy barrel swivel to the wire using a haywire twist: (1) Pass the wire through the eye of the barrel swivel and make 3 loose twists; (2) make 5 tight wraps, winding the free end of the wire around the standing wire; (3) make a right-angle bend in the free end; (4) turn the "handle" until the excess wire breaks off.*

Braided-Wire Leader. *Attach a sturdy barrel swivel to the wire by (1) threading on a metal sleeve, (2) passing the end of the wire through the swivel and then through the sleeve again, (3) passing the end through the sleeve a third time, (4) pulling on the leader to pull the loop of wire into the sleeve and (5) firmly crimping the sleeve. Repeat the procedure to attach a heavy clip to the other end of the wire.*

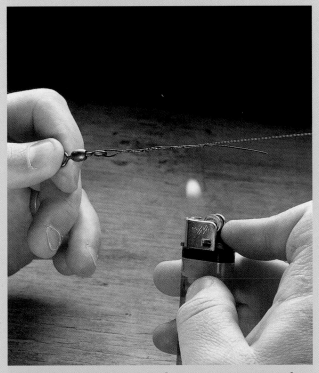

Nylon-Coated Wire. *Attach a sturdy barrel swivel to the wire using a twist-melt connection: Pass the wire through the swivel and twist it around itself about 5 times (left). Heat the twists with a lighter until the plastic just starts to melt; don't let it catch on fire (right). Trim the tag end. Repeat the procedure to attach a heavy clip to the other end of the wire.*

PIKE/MUSKIE BOATS

If you fish only on small or sheltered waters, just about any boat will do. But at some point in time, most serious pike and muskie anglers find themselves plying good-sized bodies of water such as large natural lakes, big rivers and even bays of the Great Lakes. This explains why boats with deep-V hulls are more popular than bass boats, jon boats or other boats with shallower hulls.

Some manufacturers offer "pike" boats or other boats specifically designed for pike and muskie fishing. Besides a deep-V hull from 16 to 18 feet in length, these models have an extra-wide beam, meaning lots of extra space for storing the big tackle boxes, huge landing nets, large minnow buckets and other bulky gear used in pike and muskie angling. They also feature a live well at least 50 inches long, another live well for keeping large baitfish, roomy rod lockers and casting platforms in the front and rear.

Most veteran pike and muskie anglers prefer tiller-operated boats because they're easier to control and have more open space. But on big water, there are some good arguments for console models: They're more comfortable for long-distance running and are rated for larger outboards.

It pays to select an outboard motor close to the maximum size for which the boat is rated. In addition to the gear mentioned earlier, many anglers use a smaller "kicker" motor, an electric trolling motor and the battery to run it in addition to a starting battery. If you try to get by with a smaller outboard, you may find yourself plowing water, especially when there are 2 or 3 anglers in the boat and water in the live wells.

What to Look for in a Pike/Muskie Boat (Tiller Model)

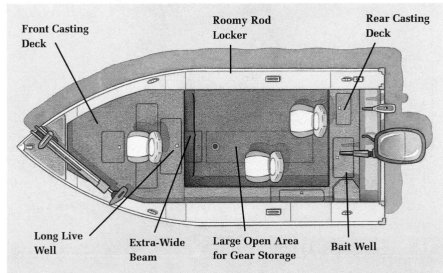

Front Casting Deck

Roomy Rod Locker

Rear Casting Deck

Long Live Well

Extra-Wide Beam

Large Open Area for Gear Storage

Bait Well

Tips for Outfitting Your Pike/Muskie Boat

Butt seats on both the front and rear casting decks take the strain off your back for a day of pitching heavy lures.

Splash guards keep you dry while backtrolling, but get in the way when you're casting. Be sure to buy the removable type that attach with thumbscrews.

Rod holders are a must for multi-line trolling. Select a model that can be adjusted to hold your rod at any angle.

A boat with tiller steering should have an electronics box that holds your depth finder, GPS, etc. in a spot where you can easily see them and protects them from rain and spray.

motor, the most important consideration is thrust. It's a good idea to buy a motor with more thrust than you think you'll need (below). Powerful motors are more efficient, meaning longer battery life, and they give you much better boat control.

For trolling presentations that require more speed, most anglers prefer a "kicker" motor, an outboard in the 5- to 15-hp class. But if you're into speed-trolling with crankbaits, you probably don't need a trolling motor at all; even a big outboard will troll down to the 4- to 6-mph speed required for this presentation.

TROLLING MOTORS

The type of trolling motor you need depends on your style of fishing. If you do a lot of casting with artificials, for example, you'll probably want a bow-mount electric motor that enables you to keep your hands free, yet holds your boat in the right position. But if you spend most of your time slow-trolling with live bait on distinct structure, a transom-mount electric gives you the precise boat control you need, even when you're fishing in a stiff wind.

When selecting an electric

Recommended Thrust

Boat Weight* (Pounds)	Pounds of Thrust
600	30
1000	40
1250	50
1500	60
2000	70 or more

Includes passengers and gear

Trolling-Motor Tips

Use a long extension handle, rather than a foot pedal, for more precise boat control. An extension handle also eliminates the breakdowns that are possible with cable steering.

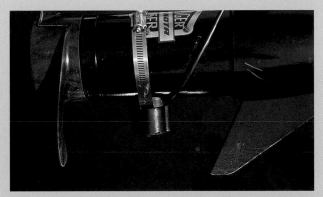

Mount the transducer of your front depth finder to the lower unit of your bow-mount trolling motor. This gives you better depth control because you're reading the depth directly below the motor, not the depth at the transom.

Many anglers outfit their boat with a pair of depth finders. The one on the console or at the rear gives you a high-speed depth reading while the one on the bow (inset) enables you keep your boat on the structure and spot fish.

ELECTRONICS

Good electronics are indispensible in pike and muskie fishing. Even if you spend most of your time working shallow, weedy water, there will be instances when the fish move to the drop-offs adjacent to weed flats or retreat to even deeper water. Without a depth finder, you would be fishing "blind."

Shallow-water fishermen who use their depth finder to find the deepest part of a weed flat or for other depth-only purposes can easily get by with a flasher. But if you're searching for fish in deeper water, a good liquid-crystal or video sounder is a much better choice. Not only will it display the fish much longer than a flasher, it will also give you surface temperature and speed readings.

A pike/muskie boat that will be used on big water should also be equipped with a GPS unit. Not only will it help you pinpoint productive fishing spots, it will get you back to the landing in foggy or stormy weather or at night. Another valuable tool on big water is a hand-held marine radio. It will enable you to call for help should problems arise, and it also makes it possible to exchange fishing information with other anglers.

For locating coldwater pockets likely to hold pike in summer, you'll need a hand-held temperature gauge (p. 138) that will give you a reading at any depth.

If you like to troll with artificials and your depth finder does not provide a speed reading, consider buying a separate trolling speed indicator. Otherwise it's difficult to control your trolling speed, especially when fishing in wind or current.

How To Catch Pike & Muskie

What to Look for in a Depth Finder

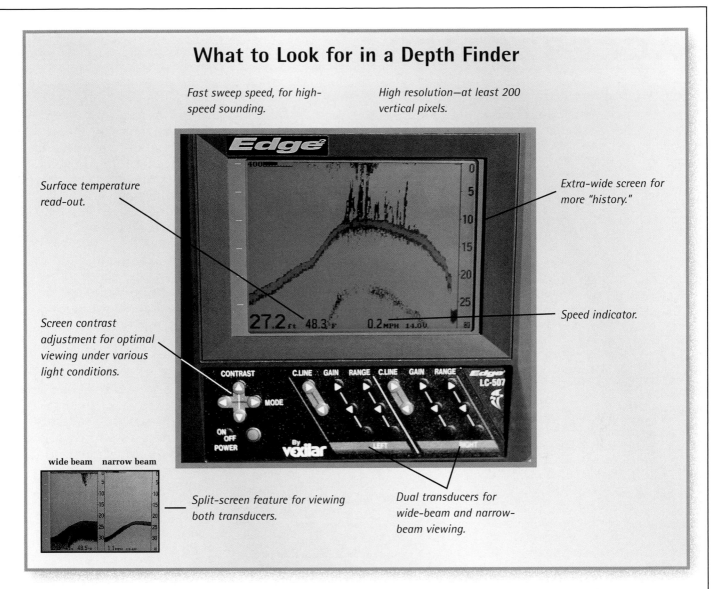

Fast sweep speed, for high-speed sounding.

High resolution—at least 200 vertical pixels.

Surface temperature read-out.

Extra-wide screen for more "history."

Speed indicator.

Screen contrast adjustment for optimal viewing under various light conditions.

wide beam   narrow beam

Split-screen feature for viewing both transducers.

Dual transducers for wide-beam and narrow-beam viewing.

Getting the Most from your Depth Finder

Use your depth finder to keep you right on the edge of submerged weeds. If you watch the screen closely, you can see the ragged fringe that indicates the weedline (arrow).

Thick marks in areas that hold panfish, perch and other smaller fish often reveal the location of a good-sized pike or muskie.

ACCESSORIES

Fishing for pike and muskies requires some specialized equipment that may not be available at your local tackle shop. But if you try to get by with the same gear you use for smaller gamefish, you're asking for problems.

For example, if you try to keep big sucker minnows in the same bucket you use for crappie minnows, most of your bait will be dead by the time you reach your fishing spot. And if you try to land a good-sized pike or muskie in an ordinary landing net, you're likely to wind up with some ripped-up mesh and no fish or, worse yet, an injured fish.

On these pages you'll find some accessories commonly used in pike and muskie fishing:

Be sure to carry a large measuring board because many waters have pike or muskie size limits. For a precise measurement, the board should have an end plate for accurately positioning the fish's head.

Use a mesh cradle to land large pike and muskies that you intend to release. A cradle prevents the fish from thrashing violently and injuring themselves.

Special nets—with extra-wide hoops, plastic-coated mesh and even a place to guide the fish through so you don't have to "scoop"—are available.

Popular Tackle Containers

Soft Pack. *This tackle storage system is gaining in popularity because it keeps your baits organized. Some anglers have as many as 10 separate boxes for different kinds of lures, but they carry only 3 or 4 of them at a time, depending on the type of fishing they're doing.*

Hanging Box. *A large, open tackle box with upright lure hangers keeps your baits separated, prevents tangling and allows them to drip-dry.*

Standard Tackle Box. *An ordinary tackle box with extra-large trays can be used for pike and muskie baits, but the hooks tend to tangle and you may have trouble finding your favorite lure when you need it.*

Tackle Tubes. *This system is ideal for bucktails and other baits that need to dry off after they have been used. Just hang your lures in the open-bottomed plastic tubes and allow the baits to drip-dry.*

How to Select a Landing Net

Choose a long-handled landing net with a rim at least 30 inches in diameter. Be sure the mesh is small (no more than 1 inch) and coated with plastic (inset). Large mesh will split the fish's fins and may break them and, if the mesh is not coated, the hooks may penetrate the fibers and cause a delay in releasing your fish.

Popular Bait Containers

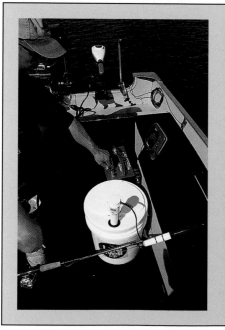

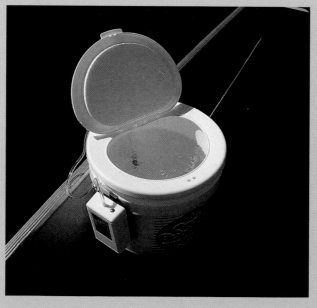

Select an insulated, aerated minnow bucket with a capacity of at least 5 gallons of water. Some buckets operate off a boat's 12-volt electrical system (left) while others are powered by flashlight batteries (right).

Jaw Spreader. *This simple spring-loaded device holds the fish's jaws open so you can easily remove hooks.*

Scale. *Select a scale with a capacity of at least 50 pounds. The most accurate scales are battery powered and give you a digital readout. Some landing nets have a scale built into the handle.*

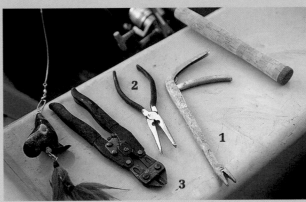

Hook Removers. *Carry (1) a hookout pliers or (2) a pair of needlenose pliers for removing deeply embedded hooks. If you can't remove the hooks without injuring the fish, use a (3) wire cutter to cut off the hook points.*

First-Aid Kit. *Accidents happen when handling these large, toothy gamefish. Should you cut your finger on the teeth or gill rakers, you'll need some adhesive bandages and first-aid cream.*

Hook File. *The large hooks on most pike/muskie lures require periodic filing to keep them needle sharp. Even hooks on new lures should be touched up before you use them.*

Glove. *A leather glove, like a lineman's glove, enables you to hand-land a big fish without risk of injuring yourself.*

LURES, BAITS & HOW TO USE THEM

*W*hen selecting lures and baits for these aggressive predators, it's best to err on the big side.

FISHING BASICS: PIKE VS. MUSKIE

Even though pike and muskies are close relatives, their temperaments differ considerably. That's why most experienced anglers will tell you that catching pike is not too difficult, but catching muskies is one of the greatest challenges in freshwater fishing.

While that assessment has some merit, it really bears a little more explanation. True—most any fisherman who tosses a lure into a shallow weedy area has a pretty good chance of hooking up to a fair-sized pike. And there are remote areas in Canada where even inexperienced anglers can catch several 20-pound-plus pike in a day. But catching trophy-caliber pike in heavily fished waters presents just as much of a challenge as catching a trophy-caliber muskie.

Perhaps the biggest difference between pike and muskies is that the latter have a habit of following your lure and then turning away just before you lift it from the water. It's not unusual for an angler to get a dozen follows in a day without a single strike. Pike show this finicky behavior on occasion, but it is not the norm. The figure-8 technique (p. 77) will turn some of these followers into biters.

Here are some other distinct differences of importance to anglers:
• Because muskies spend a considerable amount of their time in shallow water, they are much more inclined to feed on the surface than are pike. Muskies commonly swim up to take topwater baits or lures that run just beneath the surface, such as bucktail spinners. Pike occasionally hit these baits, but are more likely to strike a lure

tracking at their own level.

• Muskies are much more likely to bite at night. Until recently, most anglers assumed muskies fed on the same daylight schedule as pike, but that's not necessarily the case. While the majority of muskies are taken in daylight hours, there are times when night fishing is more effective, especially in clear lakes (pp. 142-145).

• Although there have been no definitive studies on color vision in pike and muskies, there seems to be a distinct difference. Pike are drawn to bright or fluorescent colors such as chartreuse, green and orange, while muskies are partial to dark colors like black and brown.

• Pike are more dependent on their sense of smell as proven by their liking of dead, stinky baits such as smelt and ciscoes. Muskies, on the other hand, will rarely take a dead bait.

• Muskies seem to have a longer memory than pike—or maybe it just seems that way because pike are so aggressive. It's not unusual to get bitten off by a pike and then hook the same fish later in the day. Rarely do you hear of that happening with muskies. In fact, some muskie hounds will tell you that if you hook a muskie on a certain bait and lose it, the fish is not likely to hit that bait again.

• The difference in temperature preference between pike and muskies affects the timing of "the bite." As a rule, pike fishing is excellent in early season while muskie fishing is tough. But muskies often go on a rampage during hot, muggy weather in late summer, when pike fishing is generally at its worst. The fact that muskies spawn later in spring than pike also helps explain why they turn on later in the season.

After freeze-up, pike in northern lakes find the icy water to their liking and go on the prowl, grabbing most anything you drop down an ice hole. But muskies enter a state of near-dormancy. Occasionally, you hear about an ice fishermen taking a muskie, but it's highly unusual.

• Contrary to popular belief, muskies are more predictable than pike. Almost every body of water has certain spots that provide for all of a big muskie's needs. Those spots generally hold one big fish, but it may not always be the same fish. If this dominant muskie gets caught or leaves the spot, another fish of approximately the same size often moves in. Pike, on the other hand, roam more widely. They go wherever they must to find food and a comfortable water temperature.

HOW TO TRIGGER STRIKES

When you see a muskie or pike following your bait, the tendency is to stop reeling so the fish can "catch up" with it. But that's almost always a mistake: When you slow down, the fish loses interest and swims away.

Instead of slowing down when you spot a follower, try speeding up. When the fish sees its prey trying to escape, it will often strike. Don't worry about retrieving too fast; no matter how fast you reel, it's impossible to keep your lure away from the fish once it makes up its mind to strike.

If the fish is still following at the end of your retrieve, try the figure-8 technique (opposite). How long you figure-8 depends on whether or not the fish is "hot." If it follows within a few inches of the lure and its mouth is opening and closing, keep figure-eighting as long as the fish appears interested. A fish may follow the lure for a minute or more before striking.

If the fish seems only mildly interested, however, just leave it alone, mark the spot and come back an hour or two later. By then the fish may be in a more cooperative mood. A change in the weather may also change the fish's attitude. If you see a thunderstorm approaching, for example, go back and try your spot. And be sure to try it again around sunset.

Some anglers routinely figure-8, or at least make an L-turn, at the end of every cast. It's always possible that a fish you haven't seen is following your bait, especially in low-clarity water or at night.

Figure-eighting works well with any kind of artificial lure, including jerkbaits and even topwaters. But don't figure-8 a topwater on the surface. Instead, pull it down a couple feet beneath the surface and figure-8 it just as you would a subsurface lure.

How to Figure-8

1 Reel your lure to within a foot of the rod tip and then push the tip as far below the surface as possible. The deeper you figure-8, the better the chances of getting a strike.

2 With the free-spool button pushed in and your thumb on the spool, sweep the rod in a wide, slow figure-8 pattern. If your figure-8 is too small, a big fish can't turn sharply enough to track the lure.

3 If the fish is still following but doesn't strike after 2 or 3 figure-8s, try drawing the lure across its snout. The change of motion may trigger a strike.

4 Don't set the hook until you feel the weight of the fish. Sometimes it looks like the fish has grabbed your lure, but it really hasn't. When you attempt to set, you pull the lure away and spook the fish.

ARTIFICIAL LURES

When the "bite" is on, you'll have a hard time finding a lure that pike and muskies *won't* hit. But this cooperative attitude is the exception rather than the rule, especially in muskie fishing. Most of the time, you'll have to select your lures carefully, paying close attention to the following:

Size/Shape

The size of your lure depends on the size of the fish you expect to catch. As a rule, you should use a lure about ¼ as long as the predominant fish length. For example, if most of the pike in your lake run from 4 to 6 pounds (25 to 29 inches), use lures from 6 to 7 inches in length. But if you're gunning for muskies in the 30-pound (50-inch) range, a 12-inch lure would be a better choice.

Pike are generally less fussy about lure size than muskies. It's not unusual for anglers to catch giant pike on small spinners and spoons, and even on crappie minnows. But muskies seldom exert themselves for such a small morsel.

In early spring, after a cold front or whenever the fish seem extra fussy, use smaller-than-normal lures. Gradually increase your lure size through the summer and fall to match the growth of the forage fish.

Lures with a narrow wobble or other subtle action usually work best in spring or in very clear water; those with a more intense action, in fall or in murky water. More intensity could mean a wider wobble, more noise or splash, or harder-thumping spinner blades.

It's a good idea to vary the speed and cadence of your retrieve to change the lure's action. Periodically speed up, pause a little or switch your rod from side-to-side to make the lure change direction. Even a subtle variation in action can trigger a follower to strike.

Color/Flash

When it comes to selecting lure colors for pike and muskie fishing, there are no hard-and-fast rules. But most veteran anglers will tell you that bright colors work best for pike; dark or natural ones for muskies.

While that's a good starting point, color selection is really not that simple. For example, pike in very clear waters usually prefer the same dark or natural colors that appeal to muskies. And muskies in murky water often favor the bright or fluorescent colors commonly used for pike.

Flashy lures generally work better for pike than they do for muskies. The flash from a spinner blade or spoon evidently catches the attention of pike from a distance, drawing them to the lure. But muskies seem to respond to color and action more than flash.

The best way to find the most productive color is to experiment. Change lure colors often and don't get hung up on a particular color just because it worked for you in the past.

Because pike and muskies feed primarily on long, slim-bodied baitfish such as ciscoes, suckers and yellow perch, it's not surprising that most of the lures used to catch them are long and slim as well. You can catch pike and muskies on deep-bodied crankbaits, but slim-bodied minnowbaits are usually a better choice.

Action

Just as the size of your bait should increase through the season, so should its action.

Determining the Right Color

Muskie fishermen take lure color selection seriously, as told in this old northwoods tale.

A muskie fisherman was carrying his gear down to the dock when he met a woman in a frantic state. Fifi, her toy poodle, had been swimming off the end of the dock when she heard a big splash and the little dog disappeared. "I think she was attacked by a big muskie," the distraught woman cried. The angler, trying to sound consoling, said, "My gosh, that's the most horrible thing I've ever heard. By the way, what color was Fifi?"

BUCKTAILS

These large in-line spinners get their name from their tail dressing, which consists of hair from a deer's tail or a synthetic substitute. In the hand, it may be hard to distinguish real bucktail from an imitation. But in the water, there's a definite difference. Real deer hair is hollow, making it very buoyant and giving the lure an irresistible billowing action as it moves through the water.

A bucktail typically consists of a spinner blade attached to a clevis that rotates around a sturdy wire shaft, several beads to hold the blade in position and one or more hooks dressed with hair. Some models have 2 or 3 dressed hooks to create a longer profile.

Because bucktails have unprotected hooks, they work best in waters with sparse weeds or no weeds at all. In heavy vegetation, a spinnerbait (p. 82) would be a better choice.

A 4- or 5-inch bucktail is a good choice in spring, when the water temperature is below the 60°F mark. But a 6- to 10-incher works better later in the season, in murky water or at night.

Bucktails that have an extra weight on the shaft may run as deep as 6 feet; unweighted models, only 1 to 3 feet deep. More hair, a soft-plastic trailer or a Colorado rather than willow-leaf blade also reduce the running depth. Make your selection based on the depth of the cover or structure you'll be fishing.

Bucktails are normally fished with a slow, steady retrieve which makes it easy for the fish to zero in on the bait. This, combined with the open hooks, explains why these lures give you a high hooking percentage.

Types of Bucktails

Popular types of bucktails include (1) willow-leaf models with a single dressed treble, such as the Windel's Harasser, for fishing deep and (2) Colorado-blade models with a pair of dressed trebles, such as the Buchertail, for fishing shallow. Some bucktails have an extra weight on the shaft (3) to increase running depth.

Tips for Fishing with Bucktails

Begin reeling as soon as the lure hits the water. Reel rapidly at first to make sure the blade starts spinning and then slow down a little when you feel the vibrations.

When fishing shallow weedtops, hold your rod tip high and reel rapidly. To fish deeper weeds, lower your rod tip and slow down your retrieve.

SPINNERBAITS

A spinnerbait is an excellent choice for fishing in dense weeds because the safety-pin shaft parts the vegetation and keeps the single hook from fouling. The spinning blade provides lift when you retrieve, so you can easily keep the lure riding high. But when you slow down, the heavy head makes the lure sink rapidly and causes the blade to helicopter, making it possible to work steep breaks and deep holes.

Spinnerbaits come in single- and tandem-blade models. Single-blade spinnerbaits run deepest, helicopter best and are easiest to cast. Tandem-blade models have more lift, and their stronger beat makes them a good choice for fishing at night or in discolored water.

The type of blade is also important. Willow-leaf blades, because they spin closet to the shaft, are the most weedless. But Colorado blades produce more vibration. Many tandem-blade models have a large willow leaf for the main blade and a smaller Colorado farther down the shaft.

Most of the spinnerbaits used for pike and muskie fishing weigh from ½ to 1 ounce. But in spring, the ¼- to ⅜-ounce models commonly used for bass fishing are likely to work better. Bucktail hook dressings are most popular, but you can also buy models with mylar, tinsel, live-rubber or feather dressings.

One reason spinnerbaits are so popular for pike and muskies is that they can be fished in so many different ways. Besides casting or trolling them through shallow weedy cover and helicoptering them into deeper holes, you can count them down to reach fish suspended in open water, jig them along the bottom or bulge them on the surface.

Spinnerbaiting Tips

Add a treble-hook trailer to your single hook when fishing in light cover. Slide a piece of surgical tubing over the shank of the treble and then push the single hook through the treble's eye.

Push a soft-plastic curlytail onto the hook to give your spinnerbait extra action. Make sure the end of the curlytail protrudes farther than the tail dressing.

Tandem vs. Single-Blade Spinnerbaits

Popular types of spinnerbaits include (1) tandem-blade models, for working shallow cover, and (2) single-blade models, for helicoptering and fishing deeper.

Jigs

When the going gets tough, veteran pike and muskie anglers reach for their jig boxes. They know that a jig is the best choice in cold or clear water, or whenever the fish are in a negative mood.

Jigs also work well for reaching fish in deep water or working tight spots or small pieces of structure, such as a tiny rock pile. They are not a good choice for fishing a wide expanse of cover, such as a large weed flat, because it would take too long to work the area thoroughly and find the fish. However, if you locate some fish using a faster lure like a crankbait, it's a good idea to "clean up" with a jig once the crankbait bite winds down.

Most pike/muskie jigs have a large, bulky body and are considerably heavier than the jigs used for bass and walleyes. As a rule, use a $3/8$-ounce jig head in water of 10 feet or less and add another $1/4$ ounce for each additional 10 feet. In other words, you'll need a $5/8$-ounce jig head in

dense vegetation, you'll need a cone head with the attachment eye at the front tip. An attachment eye at the top of the jig head tends to gather bits of vegetation.

Ordinarily, a weedguard is not necessary. If your jig fouls in the vegetation, just give it a sharp jerk to rip it free. The change in action may draw a fish's attention. If you prefer a weedguard, just use a weedless bass jig.

Be sure your jig head has a sturdy hook that won't straighten out from the weight of a big fish. Most mass-produced pike/muskie jigs have relatively dull hooks, so it's important to carry a hook file and sharpen them to a needle point.

The majority of pike/muskie jigs have soft-plastic dressings including shadtails, Reapers, lizards, craws and single or double curlytails. Not only are soft plastics extremely lifelike, they sink very slowly, giving the fish plenty of time to examine the lure. But some fishermen prefer a bucktail dressing because of its pulsating or breathing action.

Color selection in jig fishing is no different than in other kinds of fishing, but pike in most waters seem to favor fluorescent orange or bright red jig heads. In fact, muskie anglers often avoid red or orange heads because they attract too many pike.

How you retrieve your jig depends mainly on water temperature and the mood of the fish. In the cold water of early spring, a slow, steady retrieve with hops only a few inches high (or no hops at all) usually works best. In midsummer, however, it may take a faster retrieve with 1- to 3-foot hops followed by pauses to draw strikes. Always remember that there is no right or wrong way to work a jig. Experiment with your retrieve speed and jigging motion until you find the right combination.

20 feet of water and a ⅞ in 30 feet. You may even have to go a little heavier if you're fishing in a strong wind or current.

Head style is also important. An ordinary round jig head is the best choice for fishing in deep water because it sinks rapidly. A slider head (also called a swimmer head) works better for fishing shallow weed tops because it sinks much more slowly. In

The erratic action of a jig ripped free of the weeds often triggers a strike.

**Twin Tail with
Swimmer Head**

**Jellyhoo with
Ball Head**

**Shadtail with
Pyramid Head**

**Paddletail with
Standup Head**

**Reaper with
Bullet Head**

**Weedless Bass Jig
with Craw Trailer**

**Twistertail with
Ball Head**

**Lizard with
Standup Head**

**Bucktail Jig with
Cone Head**

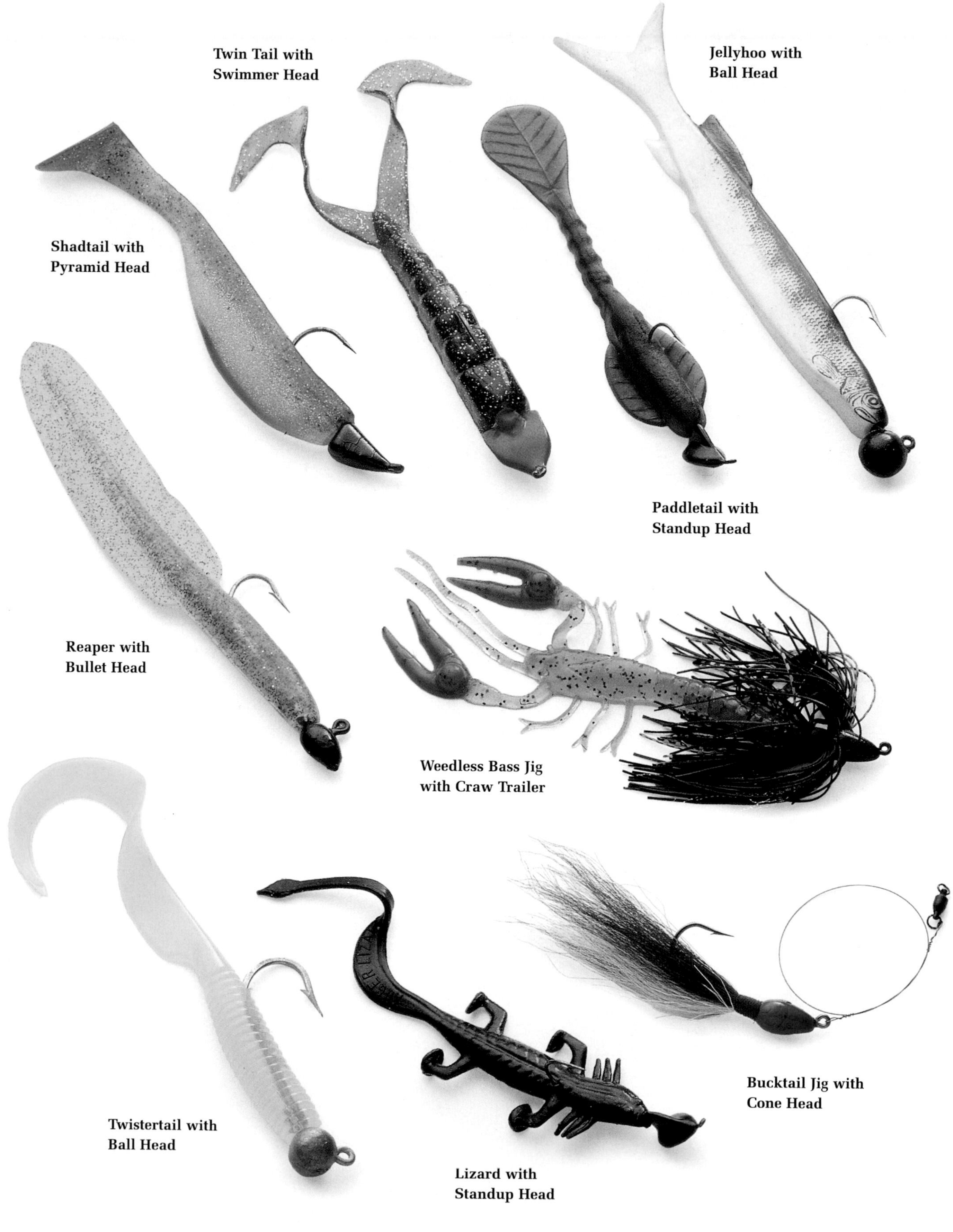

Use a hook file to sharpen your jig hook. When comparing an off-the-shelf jig hook (bottom) with a sharpened one (top), it's easy to see which one will hook the most fish.

Tip your jig with live baitfish or dead ones left over from live-bait fishing. For extra-large baitfish, you may need a "stinger" to hook short strikers. Using haywire twists (p. 61), attach a piece of stainless-steel wire to the bend of your jig hook and a size 2 to 1/0 treble hook to the other end of the wire.

When you spot a pike or muskie following your jig to boatside, don't try to figure-8. Instead, push the free-spool button and allow the jig to free-fall. The fish may strike when it sees its meal trying to escape.

To prevent bite offs, make a 6-inch "striker" from a piece of stainless-steel wire. Using haywire twists, attach the wire directly to the jig head and attach a barrel swivel to the other end of the wire. Don't tie onto a loop in the wire because the wire could cut your line.

TOPWATERS

Perhaps the most exciting moment in muskie fishing is seeing a bulge on the surface about a foot behind your topwater. You know what's going to happen next. The surface will explode and your lure will disappear.

What makes topwater fishing even more exciting is the fact that shallow-water muskies are supercharged, fighting with much greater intensity than those winched up from deep water.

Although topwaters arc used less commonly in pike fishing, they can be quite effective when the fish are in shallow water.

Topwaters are most effective at water temperatures of 60°F or higher. Although they're primarily a shallow-water bait, they sometimes draw fish to the surface from depths as great as 15 feet.

When you see a bulge on the surface just behind your topwater, keep reeling steadily or speed up a little. If you slow down, the fish will probably lose interest.

They work best in relatively calm water.

The biggest problem in fishing topwaters is missed strikes. When a follower makes a splash or swirl behind a moving topwater, the tendency is to set the hook and pull the lure away. If you resist the urge to set the hook until you're sure the fish has taken the lure, your success will improve dramatically.

There are several different types of topwaters, each with a unique action.

Buzzbaits

Buzzbaits make good "locator" lures because they can be retrieved quite rapidly. But they're lighter than most other topwaters, so it's hard to make long casts with them.

There are two kinds of buzzbaits. Safety-pin buzzers are the best choice for fishing in weedy cover because they have a shaft like that of a spinnerbait to deflect the vegetation. In-line buzzers have an exposed hook, so they work best in snag-free water.

Buzzbaits differ from other topwaters in that they sink when you stop reeling. But that makes it possible to use the "getaway" technique (p. 91) to draw more strikes.

Propbaits

As their name suggests, propbaits get their action from a propeller at one or both ends of the lure. On some models, the propeller spins the entire head or tail section.

In selecting a propbait, the main consideration is the amount of action. Models with a spinning head or tail generally have more action than those in which only the propeller spins.

The intense action is a plus in murky water, at night or on a choppy surface. But in clear or calm water, propbaits with a subtle action usually work better.

As a rule, propbaits are most effective when retrieved slowly and steadily. But it pays to mix in periodic twitches and pauses to see what the fish want on a particular day.

Stickbaits

These long, thin, tail-weighted baits create less commotion than most other topwaters, so they work best in relatively clear water. Although stickbaits have no "built-in" action, their body balance causes them to dart erratically from side-to-side when retrieved with a series of downward twitches.

Although this erratic retrieve, called "walking the dog," is very appealing to muskies and pike, the constant changing of direction makes it difficult for them to track the bait. Consequently, you can expect more missed strikes than with other kinds of topwaters.

Crawlers

No other topwater creates as much noise and surface disturbance as a crawler. The hinged arms or cupped face give the bait a distinct crawling or swimming action and produce a loud gurgling or plopping sound that attracts fish even in low-clarity water.

Crawlers are normally fished with a slow, steady retrieve, so the fish have no trouble zeroing in on the lure. This explains why crawlers are so popular among muskie night stalkers. If a steady retrieve is not working, however, try a reel-and-pause retrieve.

Popular Topwater Lures

Cisco Kid
Topper

Mouldy's Hawg
Wobbler

LeLure
Thumper

LeLure
Creeper

Slammer
Thunderhead

The "Walk-the-Dog" Stickbait Retrieve

Point your rod directly at the lure, give it a sharp downward stroke and then lift the rod to throw slack into the line. This way, the lure will dart sharply to the side (left). After the lure completes its sideways glide, give it another sharp jerk and throw slack into the line to make it dart the opposite way (right).

How To Catch Pike & Muskie

Poe's Giant Jackpot

Bucher Double Buzzer

Marv's Top Buck

Boogerman Muskie Buzz

The "Getaway" Buzzbait Retrieve

After casting, let the lure sink a little and then, with your rod tip pointing down, reel slowly so the lure runs a few inches beneath the surface (left). Halfway through your retrieve, raise your rod tip and start reeling faster to draw the lure to the surface (right). Fish usually strike just as the blades start to break water.

Topwater Tips

Use a light-wire leader when fishing with topwaters. A heavy leader or one with a big snap-swivel at the front (shown) will sink the nose of the lure, causing it to plow water and lose action.

To figure-8 a topwater, draw it well beneath the surface at boatside. A pike or muskie will rarely come up for the bait if you figure-8 it on the surface.

SUBSURFACE PLUGS

These lures have one big advantage over other types of artificials: Because subsurface plugs can be retrieved so rapidly, they make it possible to cover a tremendous amount of water in a short time.

Although these fast-moving baits attract only the most aggressive biters, they help you pinpoint fish-holding areas. Then, once the plug bite slacks off, you can continue to work these spots with slower baits to catch the more finicky fish.

To ensure that these plugs attain the desired action, attach them to a flexible, thin-wire leader that has a round-nosed snap or clip. A thick-wire leader or one with a heavy snap swivel will inhibit the wobble.

There are four major categories of subsurface plugs, each intended for a somewhat different purpose:

Minnowbaits

One of the best all-season pike and muskie lures, minnowbaits have an action that is more subtle and lifelike than that of other subsurface plugs. And their long, thin shape resembles that of many of the common pike/muskie foods.

Minnowbaits work well for casting and trolling and are normally fished with a steady retrieve that is a little slower than that used for most other plugs. But they can also be twitched on the surface like a stickbait or fished beneath the surface with an erratic stop-and-go retrieve.

Minnowbaits come in floating, sinking and neutrally buoyant models. You can buy floaters that run at depths of 2 to 20 feet, depending mainly on the size and angle of the lip. Sinkers can be counted down to reach the desired depth. Neutrally buoyant models dive when you start reeling but hold their depth when you stop. This means that you can use a stop-and-go retrieve without the bait floating up on the pause, a big advantage when the fish are not in a chasing mood.

Crankbaits

The high-speed action of a crankbait has a near-magical triggering effect on pike and muskies, especially at water temperatures above 55°F. At cooler temperatures, you'll probably do better with a minnowbait.

In selecting crankbaits, the main consideration is run-

ning depth. Shallow runners, which have a short lip angled sharply to the lengthwise plane of the body, attain depths of 6 feet or less. Deep runners, which have a long lip on the same plane as the body, dive as deep as 30 feet. Medium runners have a lip of moderate length and angle and run at intermediate depths.

Most crankbaits are highly buoyant, so you can run them over submerged weedy, woody or rocky cover without fouling or hanging up. If you feel the lure bumping the cover, just slow down or stop your retrieve and the lure will float up.

Vibrating Plugs

Pike and muskies can detect the high-frequency vibration of these thin-bodied lures in even the murkiest water.

Often called "lipless crankbaits," vibrating plugs have a much tighter wiggle than ordinary crankbaits. Some, called "rattlebaits," are heavily weighted with shot to create a rattling sound and make them sink rapidly. By making long casts and letting them sink before starting your retrieve or trolling with a lot of line, many of these lures will reach depths of 20 feet or more.

Because these lures do not have lips to collect weeds, they can be fished in sparse vegetation or worked over the weed tops. If you'll be fishing

A big rattlebait produces intense vibrations and plenty of noise.

over a shallow weed flat, select a floating model.

Trolling Plugs

Trolling is the best way to locate pike and muskies on long, uniform weedlines, on expansive flats or in unfamiliar water.

You can troll with any kind of subsurface plug, but the plugs in this category are designed specifically for that purpose. Most have a broad, flat forehead that makes them wind resistant and hard to cast, but gives them an extra-wide wobble.

Different plugs run best at different trolling speeds. A slow-trolling plug, for example, may attain the right action at a speed of only 2 mph. But a speed-trolling plug usually performs best at a speed of 5 or 6 mph. The only sure way to determine the right speed for a particular plug is to let out several feet of line and run the lure alongside the boat, changing speed while you monitor its action.

Popular Subsurface Plugs

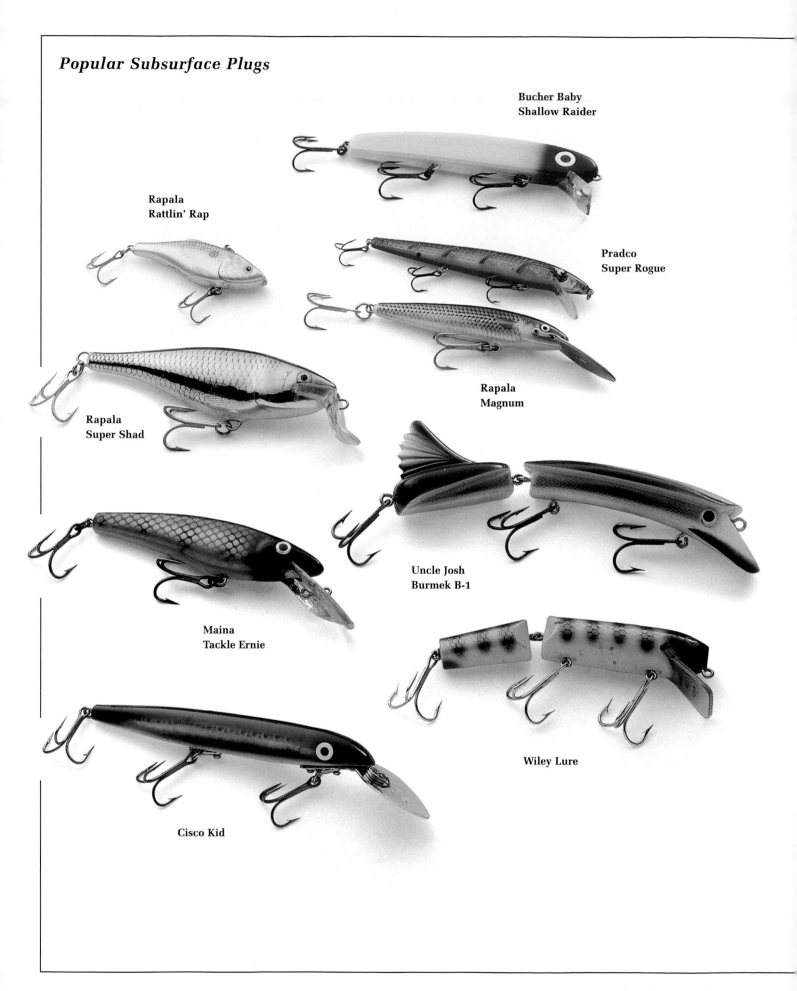

Bucher Baby
Shallow Raider

Rapala
Rattlin' Rap

Pradco
Super Rogue

Rapala
Magnum

Rapala
Super Shad

Uncle Josh
Burmek B-1

Maina
Tackle Ernie

Wiley Lure

Cisco Kid

Tips for Selecting & Using Subsurface Plugs

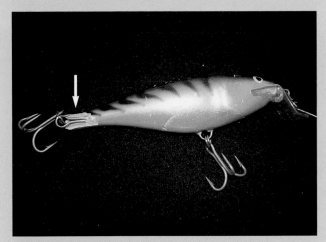

Select plugs that have an internal wire securing the hooks. Had it not been for the wire, the fish that struck this lure would have pulled out the rear hook.

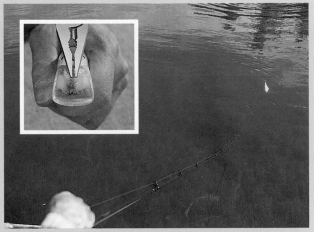

If your plug is veering to the side, "tune" it by bending the attachment eye in the opposite direction. For example, if the plug veers to the right (shown), bend the eye to the left (inset).

Hang a neutrally buoyant minnowbait in the face of a finicky pike or muskie. If you're casting, use a stop-and-go retrieve, varying the length of your pauses. If you're trolling, drop your rod tip back periodically to throw slack in the line. The hesitation often triggers a strike.

JERKBAITS

The erratic darting action of these big wooden plugs mimics that of an injured baitfish, so it's easy to understand why jerkbaits are the top choice of so many pike and muskie experts.

Jerkbaits work best under conditions where visibility is relatively high. At night or in murky water, the fish may have trouble tracking a jerkbait because of its unpre-

dictable action, so you'll miss more strikes than you otherwise would.

Unlike most other pike/muskie lures, jerkbaits have no regular, built-in action of their own; how they move through the water depends on how you work them.

Most jerkbaits float high in the water when at rest, but some are weighted to float

much lower or to be neutrally buoyant. Weighted lures run deeper and can be retrieved more slowly without floating up, so they're a good choice in cooler water. Jerkbaits fall into two major categories:

Gliders

Most gliders run just beneath the surface, veering from side-to-side with each downward stroke of your rod. This lateral movement is very appealing to the fish, but can cause problems when you're fishing in emergent vegetation. If you're trying to work a glider through a narrow slot in the bulrushes, for instance, the lure may veer too far to the side and hang up on the stems.

Divers

Divers have an angled forehead or metal tail that makes them dart downward with each stroke of the rod, so they can be fished in deeper water than gliders. Most unweighted divers can reach a depth of 4 to 6 feet; weighted ones track 2 or 3 feet deeper.

Because divers do not move laterally, they can easily be threaded through narrow slots in the weeds.

Popular Jerkbaits

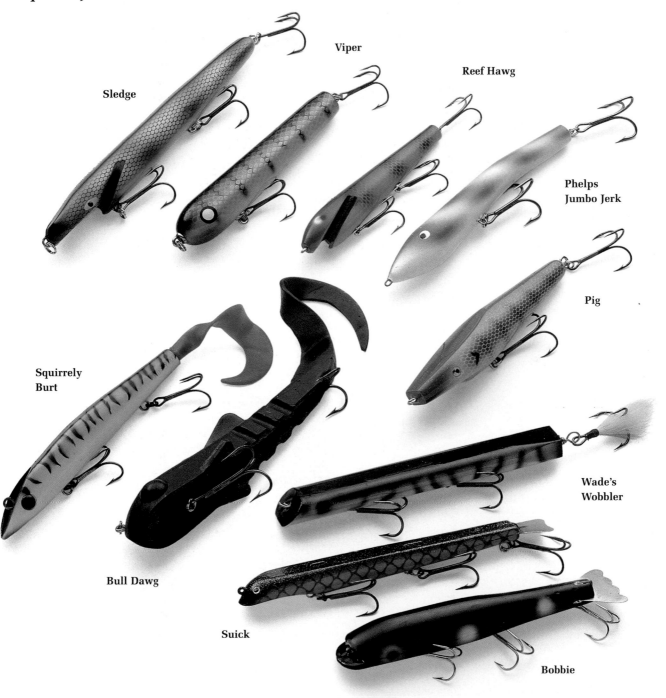

Sledge

Viper

Reef Hawg

Phelps Jumbo Jerk

Pig

Squirrely Burt

Wade's Wobbler

Bull Dawg

Suick

Bobbie

How to Work a Glider

After casting, point your rod tip at the lure and make a downward sweep of several inches to 1½ feet (left) to make the lure glide to the side (below). Before the lure finishes its glide, reel up the slack and make another downward sweep so the lure veers the opposite way. Vary the length of your sweeps until you find the action that appeals to the fish.

Top View

How to Work a Diver

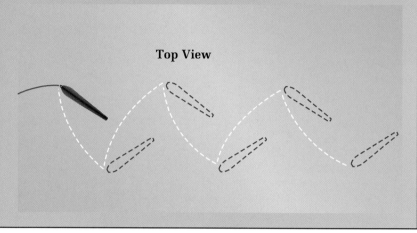

After casting, point your rod at the lure and make a downward sweep of 1½ to 3 feet (top left) to make the lure dive (top right). Then reel up the slack, hesitate for a second or two and return your rod to the original position so you can make another downward sweep. The lure will dive deeper on each successive sweep (bottom right, A-C) until it reaches its maximum running depth (D). If you want the lure to stay at a consistent depth, just hesitate longer between strokes to allow the lure to float back up a bit.

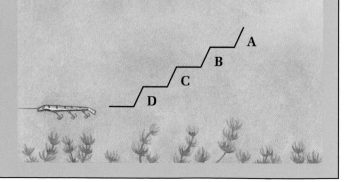

Weighting a Jerkbait

1 *After attaching sinkers to a jerkbait using double-sided tape, place it in a tub of water. Adjust the amount and placement of the weight until the lure floats with its back barely out of the water.*

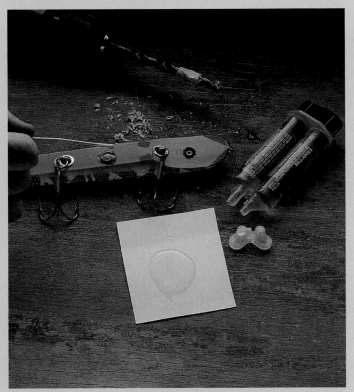

2 *Remove the lure from the water, dry it off and drill holes for the sinkers exactly where they were attached. Fill the holes with epoxy glue to seal in the sinkers.*

Jerkbaiting Tips

Bend down a diver's metal tail to make the lure go deeper. Experiment by bending the tail a little at a time to determine the best angle. But if you bend the tail too far, the lure won't dive at all.

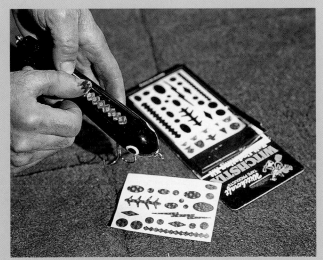

Attach a strip of bright-colored tape to the back of a glider so you can see it more easily in low-visibility situations. If you can see the lure, you're also more likely to spot a fish that is following it.

How To Catch Pike & Muskie

SPOONS

Spoons have no doubt accounted for more northern pike than any other type of lure. They are still widely used in remote areas of Canada, but their popularity has declined in heavily fished waters as anglers are switching to more realistic lures or live bait to catch "educated" pike.

Although spoons are seldom the top choice of muskie anglers, spoon fishermen are often surprised when a giant muskie grabs their offering.

Most of the spoons used for pike and muskies range from 4 to 6 inches in length, although spoons up to 12 inches long are available.

For maximum action, a spoon should be clipped onto a thin braided-wire leader, not a heavy stiff one. Always use a leader with a snap-swivel because a spoon can twist your line.

Pike/muskie anglers rely on three kinds of spoons:

Casting Spoons

These spoons have thick enough metal to provide the weight needed for lengthy casts. But don't choose an extra-thick spoon; the thicker the metal, the less the wobble.

Casting spoons can also be used for trolling and may work even better than trolling spoons for river fishing because they will stay down in the current.

Trolling Spoons

Because they're made of such thin metal, these spoons have an extra-wide wobble. Since they're too light to cast, the only practical way to fish

them is by trolling.

It takes very little speed to give a trolling spoon good action. Some models can be trolled as slowly as 1 mph but others don't have much wobble until you reach 2½ or 3 mph.

In most cases you'll want to add sinkers to your line or fish with downriggers to get these spoons to the desired depth. Without added weight, the spoons will run only a foot or two beneath the surface.

Weedless Spoons

When pike are buried in dense, weedy cover, a weedless spoon is an excellent choice. A wire, plastic or bristle weedguard protects the hook from fouling, so you can run these lures through the thickest tangle.

For fishing over very dense or matted weeds, you'll need a plastic spoon that can be skittered across the surface (p. 103). Most spoons of this type ride with the hook pointing up to further reduce the chances of fouling.

A metal spoon works best for fishing in submerged weeds. These lures are usually tipped with a pork or soft-plastic trailer, so they have an enticing, snakelike action.

A weedless metal spoon with a pork or plastic trailer has a devastating action and can be snaked through dense vegetation.

Popular Spoons for Pike & Muskie

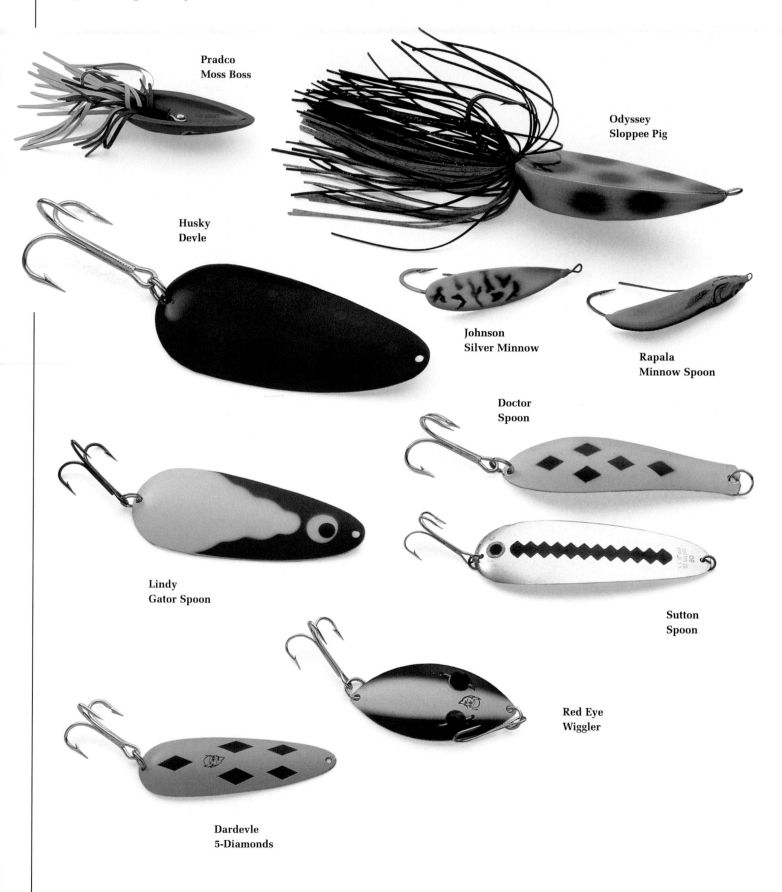

Pradco
Moss Boss

Odyssey
Sloppee Pig

Husky
Devle

Johnson
Silver Minnow

Rapala
Minnow Spoon

Doctor
Spoon

Lindy
Gator Spoon

Sutton
Spoon

Red Eye
Wiggler

Dardevle
5-Diamonds

Spoon-Fishing Tips

Add a sturdy split ring to a spoon's attachment eye if it does not already have one. This gives the spoon more action because it can swing more freely.

Skitter a plastic spoon over matted weeds by reeling fast enough to keep the spoon sliding over the vegetation with the hook pointing up.

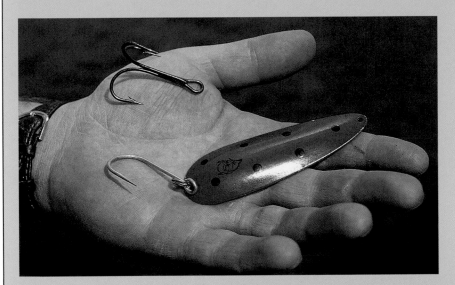

When fishing in waters with lots of pike, replace your spoon's treble hook with a single Siwash hook. The fish are not as likely to throw a Siwash and they can be released with less risk of injury.

To keep your spoons shiny and prevent the paint from chipping, keep them in a soft-pack case with plastic sleeves.

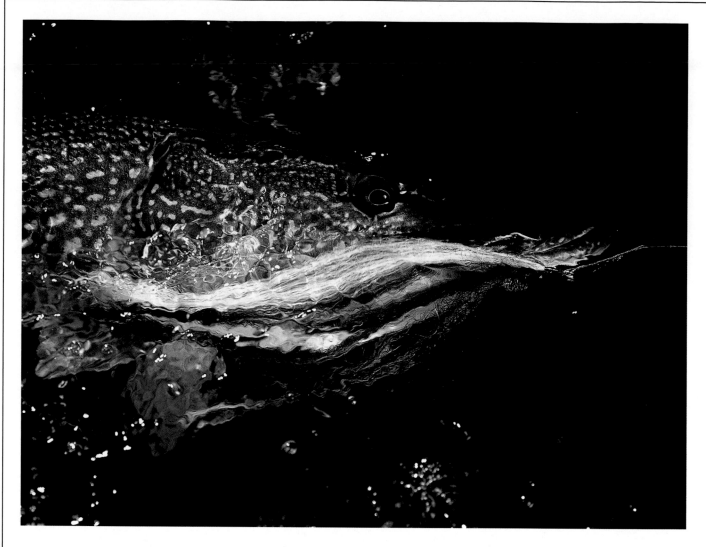

FLIES

Fly fishing for pike and muskies has graduated from a novelty sport to a highly effective fish-catching method. The big, bushy flies used for pike and muskies have an appealing action and lifelike look, so they're sometimes more effective than the conventional lures.

For example, when pike roam shallow spawning bays in early spring, they may ignore fast-moving artificials but strike a fly stripped slowly past their face.

While flies are easiest to fish in shallow water, you can use a sinking line to reach depths as great as 20 feet. You can also use weighted flies or add split shot to your leader to fish deeper. In fact, some anglers have discovered that weighted leech flies and other sinking flies are deadly when jigged along deep weedlines or over deep reefs in midsummer.

The most popular type of pike/muskie fly is a diver, which has an enticing frog-like action. When you strip, the fly dives and makes a gurgling sound as it emits an air bubble. When you pause, it floats back up. Besides divers and leech flies, other popular flies include poppers, frog and crayfish imitations and streamers, including some big saltwater patterns.

You'll need a heavy fly rod (7 to 10 weight) to handle these heavy wind-resistant flies and control such powerful fish. A floating, weight-forward line is adequate for most shallow water presentations. Most anglers use a 6- to 9-foot leader tapering from 40- to 12-pound test, along with a 12- to 18-inch "shock tippet" made of 20- to 30-pound-test plastic-coated wire.

Popular Pike & Muskie Flies

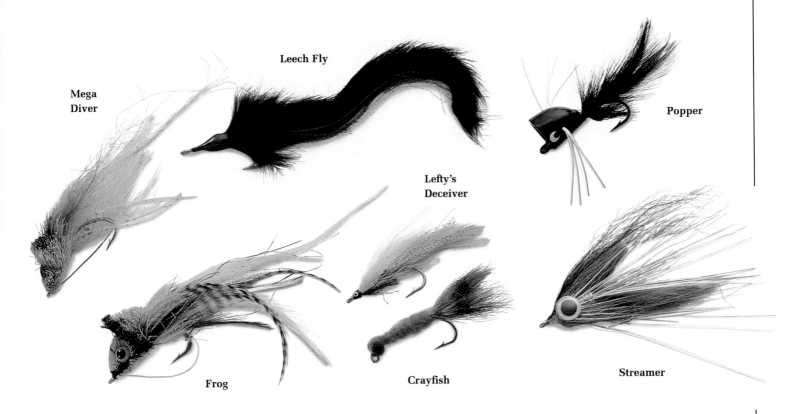

Mega Diver

Leech Fly

Popper

Lefty's Deceiver

Frog

Crayfish

Streamer

Fly-Fishing Tips

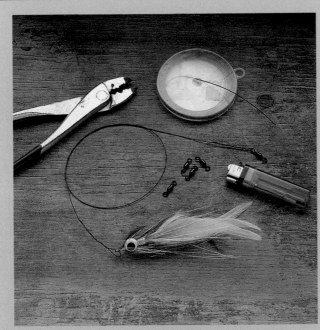

Twist-melt a plastic-coated leader with a barrel swivel at the end to each of the flies you intend to use. This way you can change flies without having to make a new twist-melt each time.

Select a fly with a mono weedguard for fishing in weedy or woody cover. The mono keeps the hook from snagging or fouling, yet does not significantly reduce your hooking percentage.

NATURAL BAIT

When you see your float bobbing wildly, get a firm grip on your fishing rod— there could be a big pike or muskie eying your minnow.

In situations where you have a pretty good idea where

the fish will be, it's hard to beat natural bait. It produces even in icy cold water or under cold-front conditions that make pike and muskies turn up their noses at most artificials.

It's not uncommon to hear about a crappie fisherman catching a huge muskie on a 2-inch minnow or a walleye fisherman hooking a giant pike on a ribbon leech. But day in and day out, large bait-

includes shiners and chubs. Smelt and ciscoes are often used as dead bait. They have very oily flesh and emit a strong odor that appeals mainly to pike.

While pike and muskies are not particularly choosy when it comes to the species of baitfish, they have distinct preferences as to size. When selecting baitfish, it's always best to err on the large side because pike and muskies do not hesitate to take a baitfish one-third of their own length. This means that fish in the 12- to 15-pound range would have no trouble swallowing a foot-long baitfish. And trophy-muskie specialists sometimes use baitfish as long as 18 inches.

Although pike and muskies will take other kinds of natural bait including nightcrawlers, jumbo leeches, frogs and waterdogs, these baits are not large enough to appeal to the biggest fish.

To keep large baitfish alive, you'll need an insulated, aerated container of adequate size. For example, if you're trying to keep a dozen 8-inch suckers for a day of fishing, choose a container that holds at least 5 gallons of water. A dozen 12-inchers require a container of at least twice that size. If you'll be fishing in hot weather, add a few ice cubes as the day progresses to keep the water temperature from rising above 60°F. Overchilling the bait, however, may kill them.

When fishing with large baitfish, many anglers make the mistake of using a hook that is too small. A size 1/0 hook, for example, is adequate for a 4- or 5-inch-bait-fish, but a 12- to 15-incher requires a size 7/0 to 10/0 hook—larger than most tackle stores carry. You may have to order these hooks through specialty catalogs.

Some pike and muskie specialists prefer to catch their own baitfish by seining, trapping or hook-and-line fishing in small streams or creeks. Wild baitfish are usually much livelier than their pond-raised, store-bought cousins.

fish are the top producers of big pike and muskies.

In most parts of the country, suckers are the number-one choice of live-bait fishermen. That's not because suckers are necessarily the best bait, it's just that suckers are easy to raise in ponds and thus widely available. Other commonly used live bait

With a light spinning outfit and a small piece of worm, you'll have almost as much fun catching your bait as catching the fish.

STILL FISHING

When you know where the fish are, no other method works as well as still fishing. Even if the fish are not feeding aggressively, their curiosity usually causes them to swim over and check out your bait. And when they do, the bait makes a frantic attempt to escape, usually triggering a strike.

There are two main still-fishing methods:

Float Fishing

This is the best choice when the fish are concentrated in a tight spot such as a pocket in the weeds, a sharp, inside turn along a weedline or a spring hole.

It's also the best way to catch fish holding at a specific depth or buried in the thick cover of a weed flat or stump field. In the latter case, you can set your float to keep your bait just above the cover, drawing the fish out of the tangle without snagging or fouling.

Be sure to select a float that's big enough to hold up a struggling baitfish. Otherwise you'll get too many "false alarms" when the bait pulls your float under. However, the float should not be so big that a fish will feel too much resistance and drop the bait.

If you're fishing in water no more than 5 feet deep, you can use a fixed float such as a clip-on or peg-on model. But to fish deeper water, you'll need a slip-float that can be reeled up to the end of the line for better castability.

A tall "cigar" float is a better choice than a round float. It not only protrudes farther from the water for better visibility, it offers less resistance when a fish pulls it under.

It's important to balance your float by adding just the right amount of weight. If your sinker is too heavy, the float will ride so low that you might not see it and the bait will constantly pull the float under. If your sinker is too light, the float won't stand up straight and will offer too much resistance.

Although most float fishermen prefer a single hook, there are times when a "quick-strike" rig is a better choice. With an extremely large (12-inch-plus) baitfish, for instance, the dual-hook setup definitely boosts your hooking percentage.

As its name suggests, a quick-strike rig makes it possible to set the hook right away when you detect a bite. This way, there is less chance that a fish will swallow the bait so deeply that it cannot be successfully released.

Bottom Fishing

When pike are cruising over a fairly clean bottom, you may be able to intercept them by "soaking" a baitfish on the bottom. The technique works best in spring, when pike are combing the shallows for food. They will take a live baitfish or a dead one, because they're accustomed to feeding on baitfish that died over the winter.

Bottom fishing is less effective for muskies. They're much less scent oriented, so they may not notice the bait, especially if it's resting on the bottom in weedy or rocky cover.

One way to make the bait more visible is to fish it on an "off-bottom" rig. The rig stays in contact with the bottom, but a float keeps the bait riding high enough that the fish can easily see it.

Common Types of Pike & Muskie Floats

Slip-floats include (1) tube-style slip-float, (2) twist-on slip-float and (3) cigar float. **Fixed floats** include (4) peg-on cork float, (5) clip-on plastic float and (6) clip-on Styrofoam float.

Popular Still-Fishing Rigs

Slip-Float Rig. *Tie a bobber stop on your line and then thread on a bead and a slip-float. Add a sinker and then tie on a 12- to 18-inch braided-wire leader. Hook the baitfish through the snout or back with with a single hook or use a quick-strike rig (below).*

Slip-Sinker Rig. *Slide an egg sinker or walking sinker onto your line and then tie on a 3-foot braided-wire leader. Hook the baitfish through the snout or tail with a single hook or use a quick-strike rig. When a fish grabs your bait, it can take line without feeling much resistance.*

Off-Bottom Rig. *Bend a piece of stainless-steel wire as shown. Then, using haywire twists, attach a bell sinker to the bottom and a single hook to the arm. Peg a float to the top to keep your bait riding well off the bottom where it is clearly visible to the fish.*

Quick-Strike Rig. *For a dead baitfish (top), insert the leading hook near the dorsal fin and the trailing hook near the pectoral fin. This way, the bait will stay upright in the water. For a live baitfish (bottom), insert the leading hook closer to the tail; as long as the bait is lively it will keep itself upright.*

Setting the Hook

When fishing with a single hook, hesitate long enough for the fish to turn the bait and swallow it headfirst before setting. Normally, that takes only 15 to 30 seconds but, with a very large baitfish, it may take 5 minutes. If you set while the baitfish is being held crosswise, odds are you'll miss the fish.

When fishing with a quick-strike rig, set the hook immediately after the strike. This way, you'll usually hook the fish in the jaw so you can easily release it. If you let the fish swallow the bait, it may be so deeply hooked that it won't survive.

Still-Fishing Tips

Make your own quick-strike rig (left) by attaching a treble hook to your leader, threading on a second treble and then securing it by heating a piece of shrink-tubing placed over the leader and hook shank. Slide the second treble as needed to fit the bait.

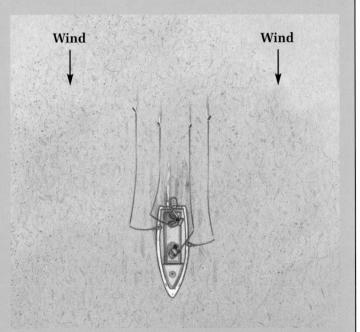

When hooking a baitfish through the snout, use a "sneck" hook, which has a squared-off bend that helps keep the bait in the corner of the hook as shown. This way, more of your hook point is exposed, improving your hooking percentage.

When float-fishing over a weed flat or other area of uniform depth, spread your lines to maximum width by placing your rods in rod holders. Let another line or two trail directly out the back of the boat. Start at the upwind side of the flat and use your trolling motor to keep the boat pointing downwind as you drift.

TROLLING, DRIFTING & CASTING

If you're the restless type that can't stand sitting back and staring at a float, here are some natural-bait methods that will keep you moving and enable you to cover more water.

Trolling

In years past, pike and muskie anglers used a simple but effective technique called "row trolling." They just tossed out a big minnow tethered to a cane pole and rowed slowly along the edge of a weedbed. When a big fish grabbed the bait and headed for cover, the anglers simply threw the pole in the water. When they came back later, the fish was completely exhausted from dragging the pole through the weeds, and a quick whack on the head put meat on the table.

Even today, many anglers consider trolling with natural bait (or artificial lures) to be unsportsmanlike. The technique requires little skill, they say, and is just too effective. These concerns have resulted in trolling bans on some premier muskie waters.

Despite its critics, trolling with natural bait is still a widely-used pike/muskie method. It works especially well for locating fish in unfamiliar waters or for working a long weedline or other long stretch of cover.

Natural bait is most commonly trolled on an ordinary slip-sinker rig but, in weedy cover, it pays to use a bullet sinker and a weedless hook (right). Some anglers prefer a spinner rig and others troll an unweighted minnow in jerkbait fashion, twitching the rod sharply to make the bait dart from side-to-side.

For the best boat control, always troll into the wind. Otherwise the wind will catch your bow and blow it sideways, making it difficult to steer. Trolling into the wind also helps control your speed.

Drifting

When you reach the upwind end of your trolling

run, simply cut the motor and drift back through your spot. To control your speed in a stiff wind, use a drift sock or slow your speed with your trolling motor. A trolling motor also comes in handy for keeping you on the right drift path. If the wind is pushing you up into the shallows, for example, periodically use the motor to kick the boat back into deeper water.

Drifting is an excellent method for covering a shallow flat where trolling may spook the fish. The basic strategy is to cover the flat by making a series of parallel drifts. At the end of each drift, swing wide of the flat as you motor upwind to get into position for the next drift.

Casting

After you find a productive area by trolling or drifting, you may want to toss out an anchor or hold your boat with your trolling motor and work the area more thoroughly by casting. You can cast with any of the rigs used for trolling and drifting or use a jig head tipped with a minnow.

One drawback to casting is that the repeated splash-downs soon kill your bait. Fortunately, pike and muskies don't really care if the bait is dead, as long as it has some action. It's a good idea to use a twitch-and-pause retrieve to mimic a dying baitfish.

Popular Trolling, Drifting & Casting Rigs

Weedless Slip-Sinker Rig (for weedy or brushy cover). *Slide a bullet sinker onto your line and then tie on a 24- to 36-inch braided-wire leader with a weedless hook. Push the hook through both lips or just the snout.*

Stinger-Hook Rig (for short strikers). *Using hay-wire twists (p. 61), attach a piece of stainless-steel wire to your main hook and then add a size 2 to 6 treble. Push the main hook through the lips or snout and the treble into the tail.*

Spinner Rig (for live baitfish less than 6" long). *Select a spinner rig with a large Colorado blade (size 6 or 7) and a single hook. Push the hook through both lips or just the snout.*

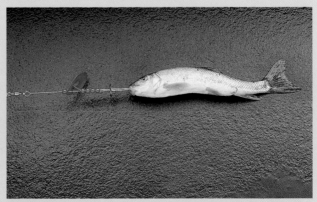

Strip-On Spinner Rig (for dead baitfish). *Push the wire shaft through the mouth and out the vent and then slip the double hook through the eye in the shaft with the points up.*

Tips for Trolling with Natural Bait

Troll an unweighted spinner rig over shallow weedtops to "call up" pike and muskies buried in the vegetation. The spinner blade provides extra lift that prevents the rig from sinking too deep and fouling.

Twitch your rod tip periodically to vary the action of your bait. The erratic movement often triggers a strike from a fish that has been following your bait.

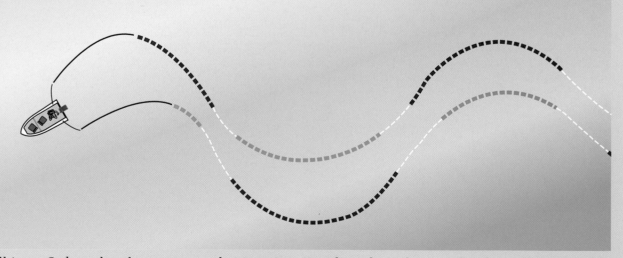

Troll in an S-shaped path to vary your bait's action. Your bait slows down and sinks on the inside turns (blue); it speeds up and rises on the outside turns (red). S-trolling also helps to minimize spooking in very clear water because the lures do not follow in the boat's wake.

Tips for Drifting & Casting with Natural Bait

When casting with artificials, use a second rod (where legal) to drift a live baitfish several feet beneath the boat. This way, a pike or muskie that follows your lure to the boat may spot the baitfish and grab it. Some anglers lower one baitfish from the bow and another from the stern and then figure-8 between the two when they spot a follower.

Attach a drift sock (sea anchor) to slow your drift speed. To keep your boat drifting perpendicular to the wind, tie the rope to the middle of your boat. Or use a pair of sea anchors, one at the bow and another at the stern.

Lob-cast your bait so it splashes down gently. Otherwise it will stay alive for only a few casts. Lob-casting also prevents the bait from tearing off the hook.

BEYOND THE BASICS

*T*here's a lot more to catching pike and muskies than heaving out a big chunk of wood or metal and reeling it in.

How To Catch Pike & Muskie

FISHING WEEDY COVER

In the majority of good pike and muskie waters, the fish spend most of their time in or near some type of weedy cover. The weeds not only produce oxygen, they provide shade, cooler water temperatures and concealment from prey.

To be a successful pike/muskie angler, you must know what kinds of vegetation the fish are using and become familiar with the most productive weed-fishing methods.

KNOW YOUR WEEDS

Experienced pike and muskie anglers know that some weeds hold a lot more fish than others. But don't get the idea that you always have to look for a certain type of plant. The fish will use whatever type of weedy cover that a particular body of water has to offer. The best weedy cover, however, usually has most of the following elements:

• **Broad Leaves.** As a rule, pike and muskies prefer broad-leaved weeds such as "cabbage" (p. 120) because they provide plenty of shade, yet are open enough that the fish can maneuver through them with ease. The fish may hang around the edges of densely matted, narrow-leaved plants, but are seldom right in the thickest part of the vegetation.

• **Proximity to Deep Water.** During the spawning period, you may find pike and muskies in shallow, weedy areas with no deep water nearby. But after they leave their spawning areas, they prefer weedy cover with easy access to deep water. That way, they can just slide a little deeper when the temperature gets too warm in the shallows or the baitfish move out.

• **Firm Bottom.** Weeds that grow on a firm sand-gravel or rocky bottom generally hold more pike and muskies than those that grow on a soft, mucky bottom. It's not that the fish really have much of a bottom preference; they just hang around the areas that have the most food.

Because a firm bottom generally has a good supply of insects and other invertebrates, it attracts plenty of small baitfish which, in turn, draw perch and other pike/muskie foods.

• **Green Leaves.** When the water cools in fall, the weeds start to deteriorate and their leaves begin to turn brown. Once this happens, they no longer produce oxygen and attract far fewer fish.

Some types of weeds turn brown earlier than others. Coontail, for example, stays green much longer than cabbage and may even stay green through the winter. And weeds that grow in deep water generally stay green longer than those growing in the shallows.

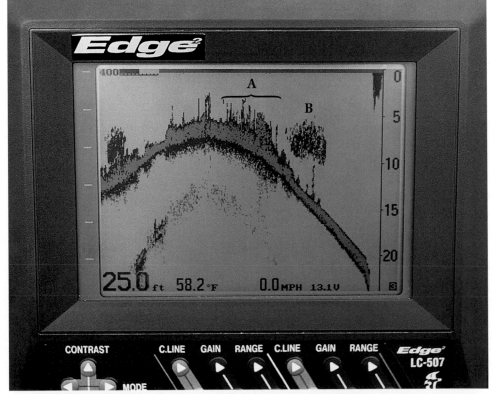

Use your depth finder to locate tall weeds (a) near deep water. The presence of baitfish schools (b) improves the odds of finding pike or muskies.

Cabbage. There are several common types of cabbage, but broad-leaved varieties such as Richardson's pondweed (inset) make even better pike/muskie cover than narrow-leaved cabbage varieties such as curled pondweed (shown). Broadleaf cabbage may grow in water as much as 14 feet deep. The leaves are more than 1 inch wide and the flowering heads often stick out of the water.

Coontail. One of the most common types of deep-water vegetation, coontail may grow to a depth of 35 feet in clearwater lakes. It usually grows on a firm bottom in dense masses up to 10 feet thick. The plants are not rooted. Coontail resembles milfoil (opposite) but the stems are green and the individual leaflets (inset) are not branched.

Milfoil. There are 13 species of milfoil in North America, including Eurasian water milfoil, an unwelcome exotic that crowds out other native aquatic plants but makes good fish cover. Milfoil differs from coontail in that the plants are rooted, the stems are usually pinkish or reddish and the individual leaflets (inset) are branched.

Bulrushes. North America has more than 50 species of bulrushes, also called "reeds" or "pencil reeds." These emergent plants have round, leafless stems that range in color from light green to dark green. They taper to a sharp point on top and may have a brownish flower at the tip. The best bulrushes grow in deep water (5 feet or more). Spike rushes (inset) grow only in shallow water and hold few fish.

Water Lilies. Called "lily pads," these floating-leaved plants provide plenty of shade and cooler water temperatures. There are 15 species in North America, with large-leaved varieties that grow in deep water (6 feet or more) attracting more fish than the small-leaved "dollar pads" (inset) that grow in shallow water. Water lilies have showy white, yellow, pink or blue flowers.

Popular Lures for Weedy Cover

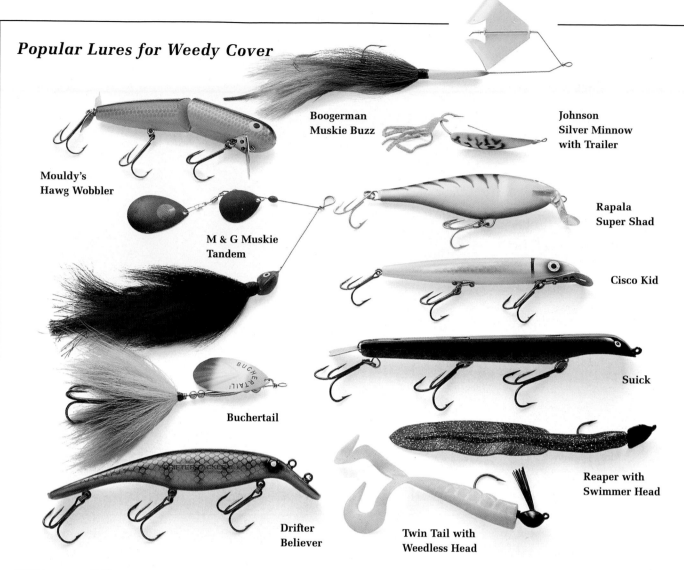

Boogerman Muskie Buzz

Johnson Silver Minnow with Trailer

Mouldy's Hawg Wobbler

M & G Muskie Tandem

Rapala Super Shad

Cisco Kid

Buchertail

Suick

Reaper with Swimmer Head

Drifter Believer

Twin Tail with Weedless Head

WEED-FISHING METHODS

To successfully extract pike and muskies from weedy cover, you'll have to match your bait and presentation to the type of weeds. Here are some suggestions for fishing various kinds of weedy cover:

Emergent & Floating-Leaved Weeds

This type of vegetation requires baits with a protected hook to prevent fouling. Popular choices include spinnerbaits, weedless spoons and brushguard jigs. If there are open slots in the vegetation, however, you can also use topwaters, bucktails, jerkbaits and other shallow runners with unprotected hooks.

Tops of Submergent Weeds

When fishing weeds with less than 2 feet of water between the weedtops and the surface, most anglers opt for topwaters or spinnerbaits. To fish slightly deeper weedtops, try shallow-running crankbaits, minnowbaits, jerkbaits, bucktails or slider-head jigs.

Lures that float up when you slow your retrieve are a good choice in this type of cover. If you start bumping the weedtops, just hesitate for a second or two and then resume reeling.

Deep Weedlines & Deep Weedy Humps

To reach fish in weedy cover more than 10 feet deep, you'll need a deep-diving crankbait, minnowbait or jerkbait. You can also count a spinnerbait or heavily-weighted bucktail down to the desired depth before beginning your retrieve.

Remember that pike and muskies are accustomed to swimming up to grab their food, so you normally don't have to get your lure to the depth of the fish.

Pockets in the Weeds

To fish a large pocket in the weeds or a sharp inside turn along a weedline, you want a lure that has good action on a slow retrieve. Toss out a weedless spoon and let it flutter down enticingly or helicopter a spinnerbait into the pocket.

You can also work a pocket (large or small) with a brush-guard jig. Fan-cast to thoroughly cover a large pocket and yo-yo the jig vertically to fish a small one. Another good way to fish a small pocket is to drop a minnow on a slip-float rig into the opening.

Large Weed Flats & Long Weedlines

When pike and muskies are scattered over an expansive weed flat or along a weedline, you have to cover a lot of water to find them. The best way to accomplish this is by "speed trolling."

Using a short, stiff rod and a sturdy level-wind reel spooled with 30- to 40-pound-test superline or braided Dacron, troll a crankbait over the weedtops or along the weed edges at a speed of 4 to 8 mph. Or, troll a bucktail with a relatively small blade at a speed of 3 to 5 mph. The fast-moving lures may trigger strikes from fish that ignore slower baits. Should you hook a weed, just snap your rod sharply to shake it off the hook.

Recommended Tackle

Whatever type of weeds you'll be fishing, be sure to spool up with heavier-than-normal line, either superline, braided Dacron or extra-tough mono from 25- to 50-pound test. Heavier line not only helps you horse the fish out of dense vegetation, it is much more resistant to abrasion from the leaves and stems. A long rod (at least 7 feet) comes in handy for guiding your lure through slots in the weeds (below).

Tips for Fishing in Weedy Cover

Use a thin wire leader when fishing in weedy cover. A thick leader would catch on the weed stems, but a thin one will shear off the stems so your lure doesn't hang up or foul.

Steer your lure through alleys in the weeds using a long rod. The extra length not only makes it easier to direct the lure, it gives you better control of a hooked fish.

FISHING WOODY COVER

Given a choice between woody and weedy cover, pike and muskies usually select the latter. But in many rivers and reservoirs, they don't have a choice. Fluctuating water levels limit growth of aquatic plants, but there are plenty of fallen trees, standing trees, stick-ups, submerged brush piles and stumps to furnish the necessary cover.

Just as the best weedy cover is adjacent to deep water, so is the best woody cover. Pike and muskies prefer woody cover that protrudes at least a few feet off

the bottom and has plenty of the fine branches still intact. Once the cover begins to deteriorate and lose these fine branches, it attracts fewer insects and baitfish, so it holds fewer fish.

There are many similarities in how you go about fishing woody and weedy cover. Fishing a shallow flat with lots of stick-ups, for example, is not much different than fishing emergent weeds. You need a lure with a protected hook such as a spinnerbait, weedless spoon or brush-guard jig. Similarly, fishing the deep edge of a timbered

flat or a deep timbered hump is a lot like fishing a deep weedline or deep weedy hump. There, your best lure choices are deep-diving crankbaits, minnowbaits or jerkbaits.

The biggest challenge in fishing woody cover is getting the fish out of the tangle before they can wrap your line around a branch. That's why some reservoir anglers use an extra-stiff rod and 50-pound-test line. Strong line has another advantage: Should you snag up, you may be able to straighten your hooks enough to pull free.

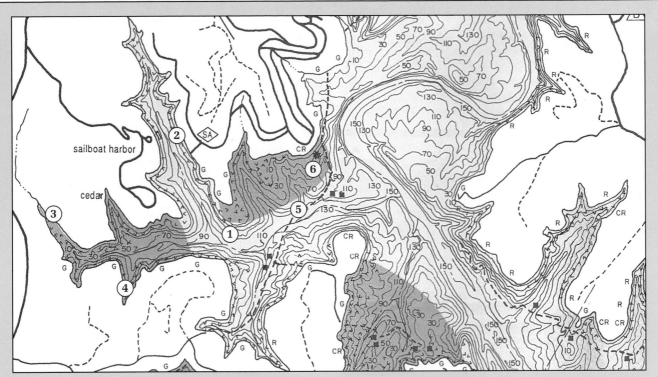

Reservoir maps reveal the location of various types of woody cover including (1) points with standing timber, (2) timbered edges of creek channels and the main river channel, (3) stump fields, (4) wooded coves, (5) roadbeds and fencelines and (6) man-made fish attractors, which may be constructed from piles of logs or clumps of branches lashed together.

Clip off the leading barbs of your treble hooks to reduce the chances of snagging up in woody cover. Some anglers use jigs and other lures with bendable wire hooks that straighten with a hard pull, but they risk losing a trophy-size fish.

Free snagged lures using a long pole with a wire pigtail on the end. When you snag up, tighten your line, put the pigtail around it and push the pole down to the lure to poke it free.

FISHING IN OPEN WATER

Pike and muskies spend a lot more time roaming open water than most anglers think, especially in very large bodies of water and in deep, clear lakes. They commonly suspend in midwater as they pursue schools of ciscoes and other pelagic (open-water) baitfish.

Although there are times when you'll find the fish suspended in the middle of nowhere, they're more often relating to something. One common pattern, for example, is suspending from 100 to 500 feet off a widely used piece of structure such as a weedline, hump or creek-channel margin. You'll normally find the fish at the same depth as those that are using the structure.

Another common pattern is suspending in the thermocline, which is the zone of rapid temperature change separating the warm surface water from the cold water in the depths. In the majority of lakes, the thermocline forms at a depth of less than 35 feet.

How you fish for open-water pike and muskies depends on their depth. When the fish are feeding on ciscoes in 30 to 50 feet of water, as they commonly do in shield lakes, the best way to catch them is by trolling with down-riggers (p. 128). You could just add enough sinkers to your line to reach those depths, but your depth control would be much less precise.

You can use most any sub-surface lure when trolling

Popular Lures for Open-Water Trolling

Bucher Depth Raider

Bomber Magnum Long "A"

Spoon Plug

Lindy Gator Spoon

Dardevle

Blue Fox Musky Buck

Original Rapala #18

Bucher Baby Tail

Maina Tackle 10" Jake

Bucher Jointed Shallow Raider

Drifter Jointed Believer

with downriggers, but there is no need for deep-diving crankbaits. Because these lures dive much deeper than your cannonball, you lose depth control, and the hard-pulling lures may trip your line releases.

Another effective deep-trolling method is wire-lining. The thin diameter of the stainless-steel wire line combined with its weight enables you to get your lures considerably deeper than you could with mono or even superline.

When the fish are in the top 10 feet, you can reach them by longline trolling with lures such as shallow-running crankbaits, minnowbaits, spoons and bucktails. Some anglers even troll with jerk-baits, periodically sweeping their rod as they troll to impart the necessary action. To reach fish in the mid-depths (10 to 30 feet), you'll need medium- to deep-running crankbaits and minnowbaits.

Although pike and muskies are not as likely to spook from the boat as most other gamefish, spooking may be a problem in ultraclear water, especially when the fish are at depths of 20 feet or less. By the time your lures get to the fish, they have moved away from the wake. But you can minimize the spooking problem and greatly increase your zone of coverage by using side planers (p. 128).

Spooking is rarely a problem in waters of low to moderate clarity. In fact, the fish often seem to be attracted by the noise and turbulence of the engine. To take advantage of this aggressive behavior, some anglers speed troll with crankbaits trailing right in the engine's propwash. Trolling speeds of up to 7 mph are not unusual.

Recommended Tackle

Downrigger Fishing: Use a medium-power trolling rod at least 8 feet long combined with a high-speed, high-capacity, level-wind reel spooled with 17- to 25-pound-test mono or superline.

Longline Trolling: Use a 6$\frac{1}{2}$- to 7$\frac{1}{2}$-foot medium-heavy to heavy-power trolling rod and a high-speed, high-capacity, level-wind reel spooled with 17- to 25-pound-test superline.

Speed Trolling: Use an extra-stiff 6- to 6$\frac{1}{2}$-foot rod with a roller guide on the tip and a high-speed, high-capacity, level-wind reel spooled with 25- to 30-pound-test stainless-steel wire line.

Trolling with Downriggers

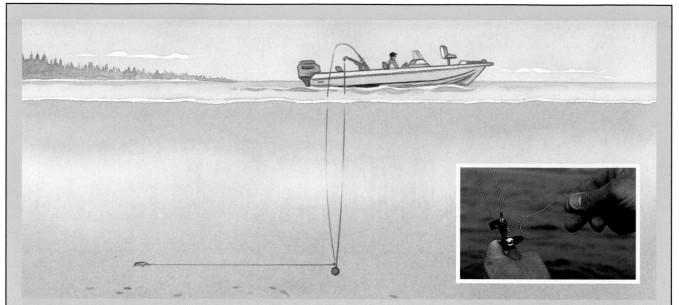

Attach your line to a release (inset) on the cannonball and then lower the cannonball to a depth slightly shallower than that where you're graphing the most baitfish. Then place your rod in a rod holder and tighten up the line enough to put a sharp bend in the rod.

Trolling with Side Planers

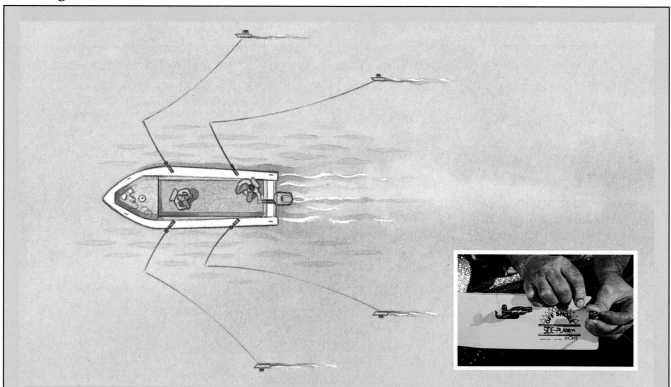

Let out line until your lure is the desired distance behind the boat and then clip a side planer (inset) onto the line. Set the board in the water and feed line until the planer is the desired distance to the side of the boat. Place your rod in a rod holder. When a fish strikes, reel in the board, detach it from the line and then reel in the fish. Some anglers troll with as many as 4 side planers set at different distances from the boat.

Speed Trolling

Let out a crankbait 30 to 40 feet and then place your rod in a rod holder. Otherwise, the strong pull would soon tire your arm. Increase your speed until the lure starts turning onto its side and coming to the surface. Then decrease the speed slightly so the lure tracks straight. Check your drag to make sure it is tight enough that it doesn't slip from the strong pull but not so tight that a fish could break your line on the strike.

Tips for Fishing in Open Water

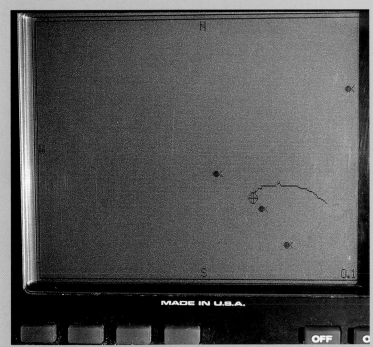

Use the plotter screen on your GPS to locate and stay in the vicinity of fish in open water. When you catch a fish or lose one, place a fish icon on the screen. Then you can easily stay in the most productive zone.

Attach your lure directly to the line when speed trolling with large plugs. The fish rarely take the lure so deeply that a wire leader is necessary, and the leader inhibits the lure's action.

COLD FRONTS

Northern pike have a reputation as being "immune" to cold fronts, but that's not really the case. It's true that small pike continue to bite through even the most severe cold-front conditions, but good-sized pike react to cold fronts in much the same way as most other gamefish. As a rule, they go deeper or bury themselves in the weeds, and feeding activity slows considerably. Muskies show an even greater reaction to cold fronts, and just a mild front can dramatically slow the action.

Pike and muskies show a fairly typical reaction to the onset and passage of a cold front. As the front is approaching, they turn on and feed heavily, and the feeding binge usually continues until the front has passed through. The next day, however, when the skies have cleared and the air temperature is 10 to 20 degrees lower, fishing gets tough. How long it stays tough depends on the severity of the front. A mild front may slow the action for only a day; a severe front, especially one accompanied by lots of thunder and lightning, 2 or even 3 days.

Nobody relishes the thought of fishing under cold-front conditions, but the situation is far from hopeless. Here are some tips that will greatly improve your chances:
• Because of the clear skies, sunlight penetrates more deeply after a cold front, so it pays to fish at least 5 or 10 feet deeper than you normally would.
• Fish in late afternoon and early evening; that's when the water temperature peaks and the fish are most active.
• Concentrate on your best spots. Cold-front days are not the time to explore new water.
• Slow down. Cold-front fish are not chasers, but they may take a nip at a lure retrieved slowly past their nose or live bait dangled in their face.
• Fish tight to the cover. Pike and muskies buried in the weeds are not likely to swim into open water to take a bait.

More Cold-Front Tips

When a severe cold front slows fishing in your favorite lake, try a nearby river. Pike and muskies in rivers seem less affected by cold fronts, probably because of the current and lower clarity water.

Cold-front pike and muskies in lakes often hold in areas with current. You'll find them in narrows, around tributaries and in other spots where the moving water concentrates baitfish.

Fish the downwind shoreline where wave action concentrates plankton and baitfish and clouds the water. Pike and muskies there will be more active than those along the lee shoreline.

Switch to smaller lures with a more subtle action under cold-front conditions. Instead of a tandem muskie spinnerbait, for instance, try a single-blade spinnerbait intended for bass.

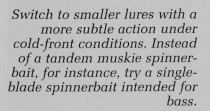

SIGHT FISHING

Although sight fishing is not the most popular pike/muskie technique, it is arguably the most exciting. Even the most seasoned anglers get shaky knees when they spot a big pike or muskie charging their lure.

Sight fishing is primarily an early season option on most waters. That's the time when the fish are most likely to be in very shallow water, and that's also the time when the water is clear enough that you can easily see them.

In many Canadian lakes, however, the fish remain in the shallows much longer and the water stays clear, so you can sight fish well into the summer.

The obvious advantage to sight fishing is that you don't waste time fishing unproductive water. You keep moving until you spot a fish and then attempt to catch it. The obvious disadvantage is that if you can see the fish, it can probably see you, so getting it to strike may not be easy.

Here are some tips that can significantly boost your sight-fishing odds:

• Wear polarized sunglasses

to minimize surface glare so you can see into the water.
• Approach the fish with the sun at your back or side to improve visibility, but try to avoid casting your shadow over the fish and spooking them.
• Wear drab clothing. If you're wearing a bright-colored shirt or cap, the fish will probably spot you before you spot them.
• Use small, lightweight lures with a subtle action and a dark or natural color. If you heave out a heavy lure, it will splash down noisily and send the fish scurrying for cover. And even if the fish don't spook from the splashdown, they'll usually spook from a lure with an action that is too intense or a color that is too bright.
• Practice underhand casting methods (pitchin' and bolo cast, p. 135) to achieve a gentle splashdown.
• If you spot a fish that you think has been spooked or just doesn't seem interested in your lure, don't keep casting to it in hopes that it will change its mind. Instead, carefully note its location and then leave it alone for a few hours. It will be a lot more likely to strike when you return.

Recommended Tackle

Use a 6 1/2- to 7-foot, medium-heavy-power baitcasting rod with a tip light enough to easily cast a 1/2-ounce lure. Match this with a narrow-spool, high-speed baitcasting reel spooled with 14- to 17-pound-test monofilament. A wide-spool reel will not cast as well with light lures, and is more likely to backlash because of the momentum of the heavier spool.

Popular Sight-Fishing Lures

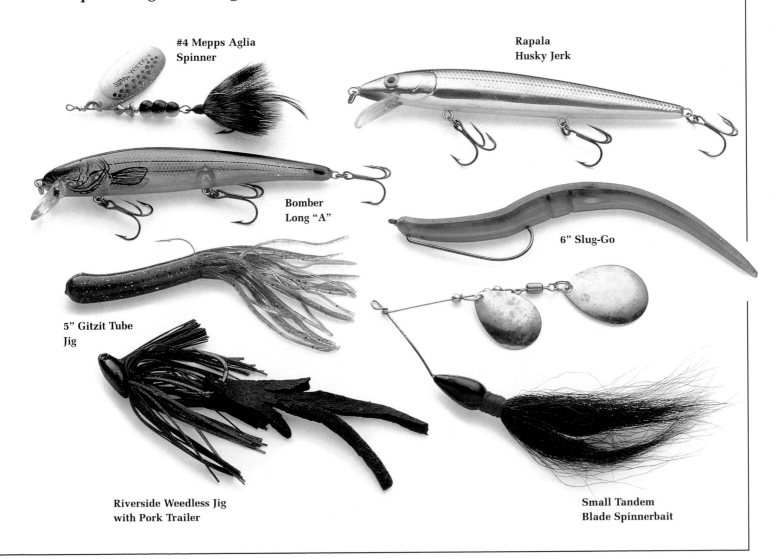

#4 Mepps Aglia Spinner

Rapala Husky Jerk

Bomber Long "A"

6" Slug-Go

5" Gitzit Tube Jig

Riverside Weedless Jig with Pork Trailer

Small Tandem Blade Spinnerbait

How to Sight Fish with a Jig

1 *Stand in the front of the boat while your partner motors you through the shallows. When you see a fish, signal immediately so your partner can stop the boat before it gets too close to the fish.*

2 *Cast well past the fish and 2 or 3 feet to the side using the pitchin' or bolo-casting technique (opposite). If you cast directly over the fish, the line falling to the water may spook it.*

3 *Begin your retrieve and watch the fish closely to see how it reacts to your lure. If the fish is "hot," maintain a steady retrieve or speed up a little to make the fish think its meal is going to escape.*

The Pitchin' Technique

1 *Strip off enough line that you can cradle a jig or Slug-Go in the palm of your hand with the head pointing in the direction you want to cast. With your reel in free-spool and the spool tension loose, hold your reel at chest level and point your rod tip slightly downward.*

2 *Sweep the rod forward and slightly upward to pull the lure out of your hand and send it toward your target. Raising the rod too high elevates the trajectory. Thumb the reel to stop the lure so it settles down softly. Because the spool tension is so loose, the reel will backlash if you don't thumb it.*

The Bolo Cast

With your lure hanging 12 to 18 inches beneath the rod tip, make a circular, underhand flip (arrow) to propel the lure toward your target. Practice keeping the lure on a low trajectory. If you lob it high into the air, it will splash down too hard and spook the fish.

Sight-Fishing Tips

Look for pike/muskie droppings around the entrances to bays. If you spot some droppings, you know that a bay has good sight-fishing potential.

Check the shady side of weed clumps and boulders for pike and muskies. In the clear water, the fish seldom hold on the sunny side of the cover.

SPRING-HOLE FISHING

Big northern pike can make themselves scarce in the heat of summer. They abandon the shallow, weedy areas that held so many fish in spring and seek out cooler water. In many warmwater rivers and lakes, they're strongly drawn to spring holes or other pockets of cold water. Muskies, on the other hand, favor warmer water and are caught only occasionally around spring holes.

The draw of cold water is most powerful in warmwater rivers or in lakes that are too shallow or fertile to have a good supply of cool, oxygenated water in the depths. In deep, well-oxygenated lakes, all the fish have to do to find cool water in summer is retreat to the depths.

Fishermen who know how to find and fish these coldwater sources catch staggering numbers of trophy pike in the heat of summer. Before getting into the details of spring-hole fishing, however, here are a few general pointers:

• **Don't Rush the Season.** Pike really don't pay much attention to spring holes and other coldwater sources until surface temperatures reach the 70-degree mark. Up to that point, you'll catch big pike in shallow weedbeds, right alongside the smaller ones. But by the time the surface water reaches 75°F, practically all the big pike have moved out of the shallows and into cold-water zones, if they exist.

If possible, try to find water at least 10 degrees cooler than the surface temperature. But if there is no water that cold, you may find pike in water only 2 or 3 degrees cooler.

Once pike are set up in the spring holes, they'll probably stay there until fall when there no longer is a temperature difference.

• **Look for Isolated Point Sources of Cold Water.** The ideal situation is where a spring or coldwater stream flows into a small bay, harbor or other isolated spot that allows the cold water to collect. If the cold water flows directly into a river, the current will carry it away and negate its effect. If it flows into the open water of a lake, the wind will mix it with the surrounding water and the temperature difference will be minimal.

• **Fish Close to the Bottom.** Because cold water is denser than warm water, it hugs the bottom, and so do the pike. Sometimes the coldwater layer from a point source is only a foot thick.

• **Calm Weather is Best.** Even in an isolated spot, windy weather causes enough mixing to disperse the cold water. When that happens, the pike leave. As a rule, pike fishermen like cool, windy, overcast weather, but for cold-water pike, you want the opposite: hot, calm, sunny weather.

Types of Coldwater Sources

Underwater springs that bubble up from the bottom form a distinct layer of cold water from a few inches to several feet thick, depending on the volume of spring flow. Because these spring holes are fed by groundwater, they're usually very cold, sometimes in the low 50s.

Trout streams and other small coldwater streams flowing into a lake or river form a cool-water plume around the stream mouth. The size and shape of the plume depends on the volume of flow, the current and the wind direction.

Spring seeps along a lakeshore or riverbank may form a small zone of cold water along the shoreline. Sometimes the spring water just seeps through the ground and all you see is a wet spot along the bank.

How to Find Spring Holes

If you don't want to invest in an electric thermometer, use a Depth-Therm, an inexpensive plastic device that traps a small volume of water from the depths and measures its temperature.

Lower the probe of an electric thermometer to the bottom and motor along very slowly. You may have to attach a weight to the probe to keep it on the bottom.

Put on shorts and tennis shoes and wade along a shallow shoreline to locate spring holes. You'll feel the temperature difference.

Look for spring holes in winter. Spring water remains at the same temperature all year, so it does not freeze up and often draws large numbers of waterfowl.

Spring-Hole Fishing Methods

When you locate a likely coldwater pocket, nothing works better than a big minnow dangling from a slip-float. Pike in cold water are sluggish and not inclined to chase fast-moving baits. The idea is to set your float to put the bait right in their face.

Before anchoring your boat, hover right over the pocket you want to fish and take a few temperature readings to determine the size and thickness of the coldwater zone.

After scoping out the cold-water zone, anchor alongside it and toss out a 9- to 12-inch baitfish hooked through the snout with a single hook or double-hooked with a quick-strike rig (p. 110). Most anglers use a sucker, because that's what is usually available, but any baitfish of that size will work.

You can also fish a deep spring hole with a deep-diving crankbait or a jig and minnow. In a shallow spring hole, try casting with a bucktail, jerkbait or shallow running crankbait. Or toss a bucktail, buzzbait or propbait

right into the spot where the cold water flows in.

Recommended Tackle

For slip-float fishing, use a 7½-foot medium-heavy to heavy power flippin' stick and a sturdy baitcasting reel spooled with 20- to 25-pound-test mono or superline. A long rod works well for lob-casting the large baits and also helps spread your lines when drifting through a good-sized spring hole.

Lures & Baits for Spring-Hole Fishing

Bucher Tandem Buzzer

Harasser Bucktail

Suick Jerkbait

Slammer Thunderhead

Bagley DB-06 Crankbait

Super Shad Rap

Jig and Sucker

Lindy Big Fin Spinnerbait

Sucker and Bobber

How to Float Fish a Spring Hole

1 *After determining the size of the coldwater zone, anchor your boat in a position that allows you to cover the entire area (dotted line). Use as many lines as is legal and spread them throughout the hole. If necessary, double anchor your boat to prevent it from swinging and tangling the lines.*

2 *When your float goes under and starts moving away, feed line until the fish stops swimming; it usually won't go far because it doesn't want to leave the cold water.*

3 *Wait a few seconds longer, reel up the slack until you feel the rod load from the weight of the fish, and set the hook. Reeling up the slack is crucial because the fish often doubles back toward the boat.*

Tips for Fishing Spring Holes

Keep the minnows that die while you're float fishing and use them for tipping jigs. For very large minnows, haywire twist a piece of stainless-steel wire and a stinger hook (size 2 to 1/0 treble) to the bend of your jig hook. Push one point of the treble into the minnow's tail.

Drift through a spring hole using a slip-float rig set to fish near the bottom while casting an artificial that tracks higher. This combination allows you to cover the heart of the coldwater zone while also catching any fish cruising the fringes.

Cast a bucktail or top-water right into a visible coldwater feeder and reel steadily to draw the lure through the coldwater plume at the mouth. If fish are present, you'll probably catch them on the first few casts.

Cover a large spring hole by slow trolling with a crankbait or minnowbait. Use a lure that runs deep enough to bump the bottom, or spool-up with lead-core line to get down. Pump the rod as you troll; the pause in action often triggers a strike.

NIGHT FISHING

Perhaps the biggest breakthrough in muskie fishing in recent years is the discovery that the fish (in certain waters) feed aggressively after dark.

Most pike fishermen consider night fishing a waste of time, and that sentiment is still shared by some muskie anglers. But night fishing for muskies is rapidly gaining in popularity, especially among anglers on waters that see heavy recreational use. There, the incessant boat traffic not only slows daytime feeding activity, it limits the areas

Productive Night-Fishing Locations

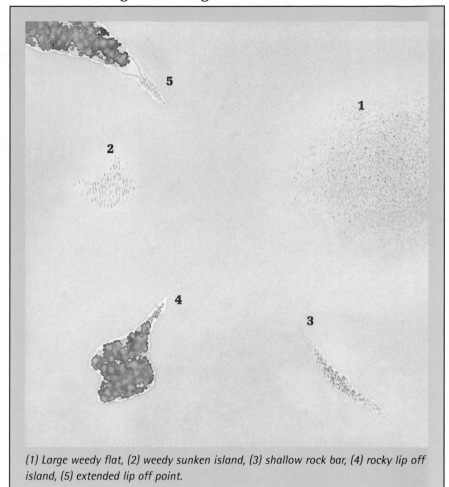

(1) Large weedy flat, (2) weedy sunken island, (3) shallow rock bar, (4) rocky lip off island, (5) extended lip off point.

you can fish and makes boat control more difficult.

Night fishermen also catch a few tiger muskies, but these pike-muskie hybrids, are not as prone to night feeding as purebred muskies.

In order for muskies to see well enough to feed at night, the water must be fairly clear.

As a rule, the clarity should be at least 3 feet and the best night-fishing lakes have a clarity at least twice that great.

The top night-fishing lakes have another important feature: lots of shallow, weedy flats or rock bars that serve as nighttime feeding areas. In lakes with a sharp-sloping shoreline, the fish usually feed during the day, so night fishing is less effective.

Night fishing kicks into high gear in midsummer and the fast action continues into early fall. The fish are most active in hot, muggy weather, especially on nights when the water is calm.

If you're planning on night fishing on an unfamiliar body of water, be sure to scout it thoroughly during the day. In fact, it's a good idea to do some preliminary scouting even on familiar waters. This way, you can mark some likely spots so you can find them more easily after dark.

If you have no idea of where to start looking for nighttime muskies, focus on the same spots where you normally find them during the day, but fish shallower. How much shallower depends on the water clarity. As a rule, the clearer the water, the more reluctant the fish will be to swim into the shallows.

LURE SELECTION

What lures you use for night fishing depends to a large degree on the wind. On a calm night, try a topwater or bulge a bucktail or spinnerbait on the surface. But when the water is choppy, you'll probably do better with a crankbait, minnowbait, rattlebait or other subsurface lure. If you prefer a topwater, make sure it has an intense action; otherwise the fish simply won't notice it on the choppy surface.

Whatever lure you select, use a steady retrieve rather than a stop-and-go or any other kind of erratic retrieve. The fish may have trouble zeroing in on a lure moving up-and-down or side-to-side.

Color choice for night fishing is a hotly debated topic. Some night stalkers swear by black lures, but others say color makes little difference because all the fish see is the lure's silhouette against the surface.

Popular Night-Fishing Lures

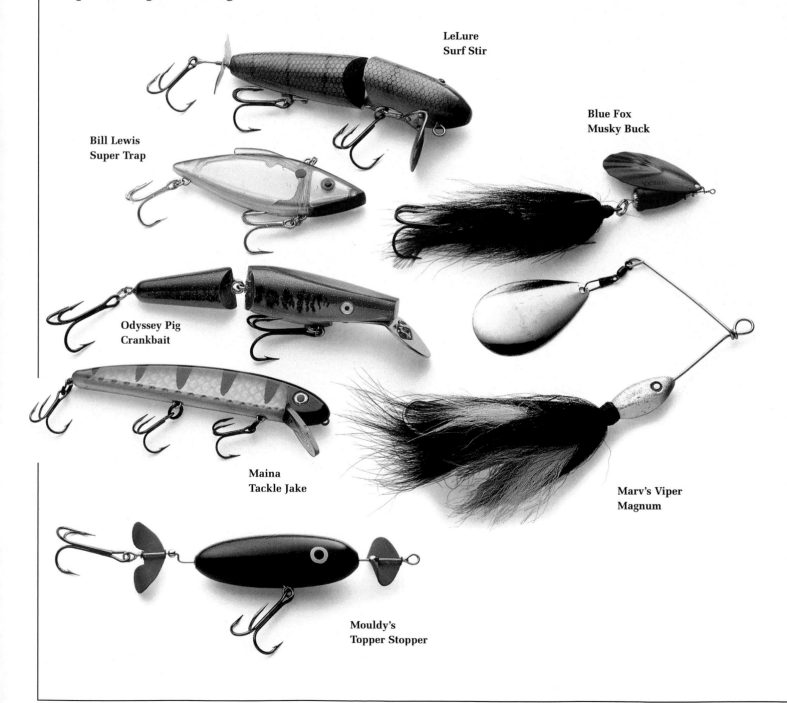

LeLure
Surf Stir

Blue Fox
Musky Buck

Bill Lewis
Super Trap

Odyssey Pig
Crankbait

Maina
Tackle Jake

Marv's Viper
Magnum

Mouldy's
Topper Stopper

How To Catch Pike & Muskie

Night-Fishing Tips

Set markers on your prime spots during daylight hours and then use a powerful spotlight to locate them after dark.

Use a battery powered headlamp to help you see follows and land your fish. A brighter light may spook any fish following your lure.

Arrange your equipment neatly to avoid unnecessary tangles or accidents. Keep an extra rod handy just in case problems arise.

If possible, start fishing weedy flats, points or rock bars close to the west shore of the lake. These spots fall under shadow before similar spots on the east shore, so any fish using them are likely to turn on earlier.

ICE FISHING

When you spot a "flag" and race over to your tip-up to find the spool spinning wildly, it's easy to understand why so many north country anglers are hooked on ice-fishing for pike.

If the spinning spool doesn't get you excited, the battle that ensues definitely will. When you set the hook, a good-sized pike usually

preference for cooler water temperatures. Anglers catch an occasional muskie through the ice, but few target them intentionally.

Here are some pointers for finding and catching wintertime pike.

LOCATING PIKE

Catching pike through the ice is easy—if you know where to find them. In most natural lakes, shallow bays are key early-winter spots, especially if they have plenty of green weeds. If you're not sure which bays have green weeds, do some scouting just before freeze up. If the weeds are green then, they'll still be green after the ice forms. You can also find the green weeds by looking down your holes or using an underwater camera.

Some pike, usually the smaller ones, stay in these shallow bays all winter. But within a few weeks, the bigger pike retreat to deeper water where they concentrate around deep points, humps or rock piles.

In fertile lakes where oxygen levels sag considerably as the winter progresses, you'll often find the pike right under the ice because that's where the oxygen level is the highest. Later in the winter, when meltwater rejuvenates oxygen levels, the fish move back into the same shallow bays where you found them in early season.

Many big-river systems also offer excellent ice fishing for pike. Just as weedy bays are the key early- and late-season locations in natural lakes, weedy backwaters are the early- and late-season focal points in rivers. In midwinter, the fish generally move into deep, slow-moving areas of the main channel where oxygen levels are higher.

Wintertime Pike Locations in Natural Lakes

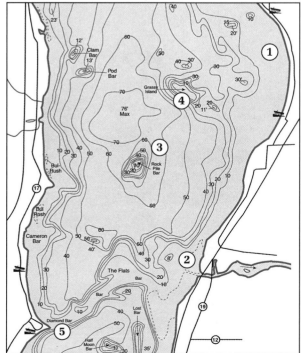

In early and late winter, look for pike in (1) shallow bays or on (2) shallow weed flats. In midwinter, you'll find them around (3) rock piles, (4) weedy humps or (5) lips of deep points.

makes several sizzling runs before you can work it back to the hole.

Unlike muskies, pike remain quite active during the winter. The difference can be explained by the pike's

JIGGING

Old-time ice fishermen often jigged for pike with a stick, some heavy braided-nylon line and a big, flashy spoon. When a fish hit, they simply jerked it through the hole and clunked it on the head. The method may not have been sporting, but it was highly effective.

Today, jigging for pike is far less popular than tip-up fishing, but it offers one major advantage: You can easily jump from hole to hole without having to adjust your depth. Some anglers locate the fish by jigging and then scatter tip-ups around productive areas.

The ideal jigging outfit consists of a stiff 36- to 42-inch jigging rod and a baitcasting reel spooled with 20-pound-test braided Dacron or superline. Be sure to attach a 6- to 12-inch, 20-pound-test braided wire leader.

Any good-sized jigging lure will work, including jigging spoons, airplane jigs, swimming minnows and plain lead heads. Tip them with a whole minnow, a minnow head or baitfish strips (p. 151).

TIP-UP FISHING

Serious ice fishermen rely heavily on good-sized baitfish (live or dead) to catch pike. Baitfish can be fished beneath a float, but most anglers prefer tip-ups (opposite), which have a spring-loaded flag to signal bites from a distance. Here's why tip-ups are so popular:
• A tip-up has an underwater spool that will not freeze up, even if your hole freezes solid. A float would freeze into the ice in cold weather so a fish would not be able to pull it under.
• Because you can spot a flag from hundreds of feet away, tip-ups enable you to cover a wide expanse of water. Where multiple lines are legal, a

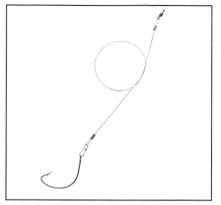

Basic Tip-Up Rig. *Tie a 12- to 18-inch braided-wire leader (20- to 30-pound test) to your line and clip on a single hook. Push the hook through the snout or back of a live baitfish.*

group of anglers can spread out their tip-ups to cover a weedy bay, a sunken island or a broad weed flat.
• Most good tip-ups have a tension adjustment that allows you to use baitfish up to a foot long without tripping the flag.
• When a pike takes the bait, the underwater spool spins easily so the fish can take line without feeling resistance.

Tip-ups are usually spooled with 25- to 40-pound-test Dacron or superline, although some anglers prefer specially designed tip-up line, which has a thin plastic coating to minimize freeze-up problems.

Any kind of baitfish will work, but most anglers use lively suckers, chubs or shiners from 5 to 12 inches long. Hook them through the snout or back with a single hook or use a quick-strike rig, just as you would for open-water fishing (p. 110). In midwinter, when the fish are less active, try a dead smelt or cisco hooked through the back with a single hook. Or use a quick-strike rig or Swedish hook (p. 151) so the bait rides in a natural horizontal position.

Popular Jigging Lures

Popular jigging lures for ice fishing include (1) Fireball jig with stinger tipped with minnow, (2) airplane jig tipped with minnow, (3) jigging Rapala, and (4) Buck-Shot Rattle Spoon.

Anatomy of a Tip-Up

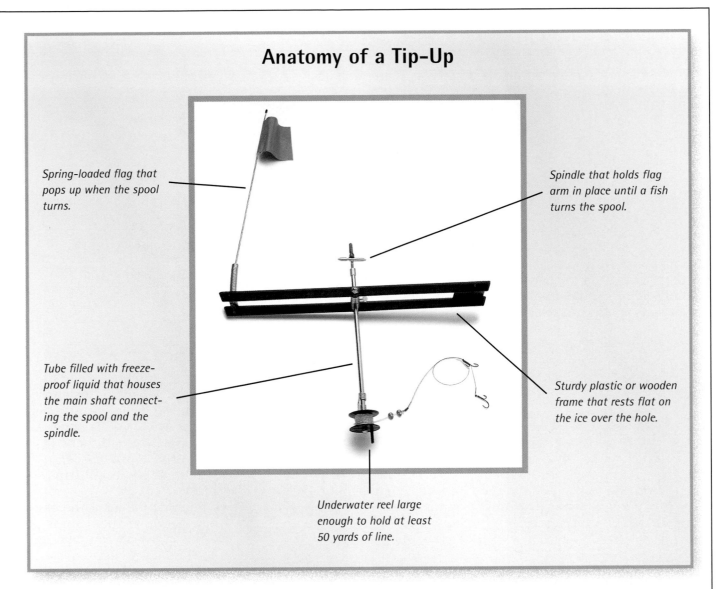

Spring-loaded flag that pops up when the spool turns.

Spindle that holds flag arm in place until a fish turns the spool.

Tube filled with freeze-proof liquid that houses the main shaft connecting the spool and the spindle.

Sturdy plastic or wooden frame that rests flat on the ice over the hole.

Underwater reel large enough to hold at least 50 yards of line.

Other Kinds of Tips-Ups

Magnetic tip-ups have a magnet on the reel (a) that pulls on another magnet on the spring-loaded flag shaft. By loosening the thumb screw (b) and adjusting the distance between the 2 magnets, you can change the release tension.

An economy tip-up has thin wooden cross-bars that fold up for storage and a flag that stands tall on a "corset-stay" type spring. But there is no tension adjustment to prevent an active baitfish from tripping the flag.

1 Drill or chop a hole at least 9 inches in diameter and clear away all the slush before setting your tip-up. This way the line won't catch on the ice chips. Tapering the bottom of the hole outward with a chisel makes landing the fish much easier.

2 After lowering your bait to the desired depth, set the flag arm under the spindle. If you're using an extra-large baitfish and want more trip tension, set the arm in the slot on the spindle (arrow).

3 When you spot a flag, get to your tip-up in a hurry. Wait until the spindle stops turning, then pull the tip-up out of the hole, grab the line and gently tighten it up to see if the fish is still there.

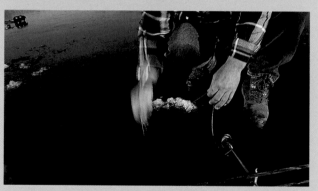

4 Pull in any slack and then set the hook with a firm wrist snap. Keep steady tension on the fish, letting line slide through your fingers when it runs. As you pull the fish back, pile the line neatly so it doesn't tangle if the fish makes another run.

5 Carefully lead the pike into the hole and then grab it across the back of the head to land it. Toss it well to the side of the hole; otherwise it might flop back down the hole when you remove the hook. If you plan on keeping the fish, you could land it with a gaff.

Use a wind tip-up to give your bait more action. Wind blowing on the metal plate (arrow) moves the arm up and down, and a bite trips the flag. Wind tip-ups work best in above-freezing temperatures; otherwise, the line may freeze into the ice.

Rig a dead smelt or cisco on a Swedish hook by first pushing the hook point into the vent (top). Then turn the shank up and push the point through the back at the base of the head (bottom).

Add a spinner blade to your leader for extra attraction. Cut the leader, slide on a clevis and blade and then reattach the hook using a crimp or twist-melt. The convex side of the blade should face the hook; this way the blade will spin as the baitfish swims.

Tip the treble hook of a jigging spoon with strips of perch or other small fish caught incidentally while jigging. The enticing action, combined with the smell of natural forage, is often more appealing than minnows from a bait shop.

TROPHY FISHING

When you turn on your TV set and see anglers heaving foot-long plugs and hauling in four-foot-long pike and muskies, you might get the idea that catching these giant fish is a snap.

And it may well be a snap—if you're fishing in remote areas of Canada or a few secret lakes in the lower 48—the spots where most TV anglers do their filming.

But what about the average fisherman who doesn't have "inside" information or can't afford to spend thousands of dollars on a fly-in trip to pursue lunkers that have rarely if ever seen a lure?

Here are some tips that will help you catch the pike or muskie of a lifetime:

• **Do Your Homework.** You can't catch big fish in waters that don't have them, so your first challenge is doing some research to determine which waters in your area have the best trophy potential. Ask your local fisheries manager about any waters with a reputation for producing big fish or where lots of big fish have been caught in test nets.

If you have access to the internet, there is a surprising amount of information available on your state conservation agency's web site and on the web sites of numerous fishing clubs and organizations such as Muskies, Inc. (p. 153).

Local bait and tackle shops

Tips for Finding Pike & Muskie Hotspots

Fishing magazines and publications of state natural resources agencies often provide valuable clues that will help you find trophy pike/muskie waters.

Web sites of fishing clubs offer information on waters with good trophy potential, and may even give you some tips on lure selection.

Muskie Magazine, a publication of Muskies, Inc. (the country's largest muskie-fishing organization), is full of current information on productive waters, new techniques and other valuable tips. (See p. ii for information on how to contact Muskies, Inc.)

True Fish Tales

Reports from around the state list the following anglers who hooked top fish in Minnesota waters. To enter qualified catches write to True Fish Tales, Star Tribune, 425 Portland Av., Minneapolis, MN, 55488, or fax to (612) 673-7774. Minimum weights for listings are: walleye, 9 pounds; northern pike 15 pounds; smallmouth bass, 4 pounds; largemouth bass, 5 pounds; crappie, 2 pounds; bluegill, 1 pound, 6 ounces; brown trout, 3 pounds; rainbow trout, 3 pounds; brook trout, 2 pounds; lake trout, 10 pounds; muskie, 20 pounds; catfish, 15 pounds. Minimum inches for released fish are: walleye, 28 inches; northern pike, 38 inches; smallmouth bass, 18 inches; largemouth bass, 20 inches; muskie, 45 inches; lake trout, 25 inches. Hometowns are in Minnesota unless otherwise noted.

Smallmouth bass

22 inches	Saganaga	Dave Mattson	Burnsville
21 inches	Lac La Croix	Torrey Swanson	Stacy
20½ inches	Vermilion	James Melson	Cottage Grove
20 inches	Vermilion	Mike Mundell	Indianapolis, Ind.
20 inches	Vermilion	Geneine Mundell	Indianapolis, Ind.
19¾ inches	Minnetonka	Todd Mauren	Burnsville

Northern pike

43 inches	Vermilion	Ed Erickson	New Hope
40 inches	Ada	John J. White	St. Paul
40 inches	Leech	Richard Wolske	Remer
39 inches	Vermilion	Dick Livingstone	Hastings
38 inches	Fourtown	Jerry Casey	Chisholm

Local outdoor newspapers give you up-to-date reports on where big pike and muskies are being caught in your area.

can also point you in the right direction, as can outdoor newspapers that cover the fishing action in your area. If you're really serious about boating a trophy, join a fishing club that conducts tournaments or outings on prime pike or muskie waters.
• **Fish at Peak Times.** As a rule, your best chances of catching a big pike are in spring or fall, when the water is below 65°F. As the water warms, big pike get more and more lethargic. If you want to catch big pike in the heat of summer, you'll have to find a spring hole or some deep, well-oxygenated water.

Muskies, on the other hand, seldom turn on until the water warms to the mid 60s, and many muskie experts wait for water temperatures to peak in summer before they start getting serious. In fact, some of the best muskie bites ever seen have come after several days or weeks of extremely hot, still, humid weather.

Despite cooling temperatures, muskies in most waters continue to bite well into the fall. A glance at the list of world line-class-record muskies (below) compiled by the National Fresh Water Fishing Hall of Fame reveals that 9 of the 17 entries were caught in September or October. And the current all-tackle world record (69 pounds, 11 ounces) was caught on October 20th.

• **Think Deep.** Although most anglers associate pike and muskies with shallow, weedy water, that can be a mistake if you want to catch trophy-caliber fish.

Many trophy-muskie specialists will tell you that the biggest fish spend most of their time in deep water. These anglers do more trolling than casting, because trolling keeps their lure in deep water a greater percentage of the time.

Deep trolling is also a dynamite method for giant pike, especially in deep, clear lakes that have a good supply of open-water forage, such as ciscoes. In Canadian shield lakes, it's not unusual to find pike at depth of 30 to 50 feet in summer and fall, and they may go considerably deeper. For example, netters on Ontario's Lake Nipigon have caught pike at depths of more than 100 feet.

Some trophy pike and muskie hounds will tell you that they catch plenty of big fish around shallow weedbeds, but those weedbeds are most likely adjacent to deep water. As a rule, pike and muskies prefer weedbeds that offer easy deep-water access to those that are far from any deep water.

• **Fish Big Waters.** Although a small lake or stream will occasionally cough up a trophy-class pike or muskie, your odds of hooking big fish are considerably better in big water.

Biologists have long known of the "fish-bowl" effect that limits the growth of fish in small bodies of water. Just as a goldfish in a small fishbowl will not grow as large as one in a big bowl, fish in a small lake are less likely to reach trophy size than those in a big lake.

There's another reason trophies are harder to come by in smaller waters. On a per-acre basis, small bodies of water generally see more fishing pressure than large ones, so any trophy fish are soon removed.

The record books confirm the big-water connection. The world-record muskie was

Muskie Records

Line Class	Fish Weight	Angler	Location	Date
All	69-11	Louis Spray	Chippewa Flowage, Wisconsin, USA	10-20-49
2 lb.	19-4	Paul Gravunder	Chippewa Flowage, Wisconsin, USA	6-26-90
4 lb.	41-0	Paul R. Obry	Cisco Chain, Wisconsin, USA	9-26-98
6 lb.	50-0	Robert W. La May	High Falls Flowage, Wisconsin, USA	10-18-83
8 lb.	50-3	John M. Vaughn	St. Lawrence River, New York, USA	6-5-90
10 lb.	45-0	Robert J. Krencisz	Middle McKenzie Lake, Wisconsin, USA	10-21-83
12 lb.	44-7	John Herman	Trout Lake, Wisconsin, USA	6-14-89
14 lb.	37-0	David Nevinski	Wabigoon Lake, Ontario, Canada	6-26-87
15 lb.	42-7	Gus Tzavaras	Flambeau Chain, Wisconsin, USA	7-8-98
16 lb.	41-4	John Sparbel	Lake Wausau, Wisconsin, USA	10-24-93
17 lb.	44-7	Rick Kaminski	Big Crawling Stone, Wisconsin, USA	6-28-78
20 lb.	50-4	Robert G. Grutt	Big Round Lake, Wisconsin, USA	6-10-89
25 lb.	55-0	Steven Albers	Eagle Lake, Ontario, Canada	9-22-85
30 lb.	51-14	Karl Dobmeier	Lake Bemidji, Minnesota, USA	9-14-96
36 lb.	51-0	Gene Allen	Flambeau Lake, Wisconsin, USA	9-21-75
40 lb.	48-8	Jerry K. Nelson	Round Lake, Wisconsin, USA	10-30-93
45 lb.	48-8	Marvin C. Bray	Big Sissabagama Lake, Wisconsin, USA	7-23-77
50 lb.	44-4	Larry A. Ramsell	Eagle Lake, Ontario, Canada	9-29-88
Unlimited*	67-8	Cal Johnson	Lac Courte Oreilles, Wisconsin, USA	7-24-49
Unlimited*	70-0	Robert Malo	Middle Eau Claire Lake, Wisconsin, USA	6-6-54

*Not recognized as hook-and-line records

When a big pike or muskie sinks its teeth into a wooden lure, it takes a powerful rod to break its grip and set the hooks.

caught in the Chippewa Flowage, a 15,300-acre reservoir in northern Wisconsin; the Canadian record muskie (65 pounds), in a tributary of Lake Huron's Georgian Bay, the largest of all Great Lakes bays. The North American record pike (46 pounds, 2 ounces) was caught in New York's 22,000-acre Sacandaga Reservoir.

There is one important exception to the big-water connection. Lakes of only a few hundred acres with a good population of trout or other salmonids have been known to produce good numbers of big pike and, in some cases, muskies. The fish grow much faster than normal on the high-fat forage.

• **Use Big Baits.** Big pike and muskies are inherently lazy. They would rather eat one huge meal than a dozen small ones. That's why it's not unusual to see a giant pike or muskie swimming around with the tail of a fish half its own length sticking out of its mouth.

It may seem ridiculous to tie on a foot-long plug, but a lure that size is really not that outlandish when you consider that a 4-foot pike or muskie could handle a baitfish twice that size. This explains why some trophy hunters think even bigger, preferring live baitfish from 15 to 20 inches in length.

Keep in mind, however, that there are exceptions to the big bait-big fish principle. For example, in waters where small shiners or perch are the predominant forage, a 6-inch lure will often outproduce a 12-incher. Smaller lures are also effective under cold-front conditions or in very clear water.

• **Use Heavy Tackle.** Casting lures and baits this size, setting the hook and controlling the fish requires heavier-than-normal tackle. If your rod is too light, it will flex too much on the backcast, so you'll lose distance. And when a fish clamps down on the lure, you won't have the power to break its grip and sink the hooks. It's a good idea to invest in an extra-stiff rod and a heavy-duty reel and spool it up with line of at least 50-pound test.

Heavy tackle serves another even more important purpose: It enables you to fight and land the fish quickly, minimizing stress and reducing the buildup of lactic acid in the bloodstream. To land a huge fish on light tackle, you would have to fight it to the point where the lactic acid level was so high that it would never recover enough for a successful release.

INDEX

A

All-purpose outfit, 55
Artificial lures. *See* Lures
Asian pike
    weight of, 18

B

Bagley DB-06 crankbait, 139
Bait, natural, 106–107
    big bait for trophy fish, 155
    casting with, 113, 115
    catching own, 107
    drifting with, 112, 113, 115
    hooks and, 107
    keeping alive, 107
    popular type of, 107
    size of, 107
    tipping jigs with, 87
    trolling with, 112, 114
Baitcasting reel, 57
    features in good, 57
Bait containers, 70
Baitfish. *See also* Natural Bait
    for ice fishing, 148
    spring-hole fishing and, 139
Barred muskie, 14
Bill Lewis Super Trap, 144
Blue Fox Musky Buck, 127, 144
Boats, 64–65
Bobbie, 97
Bolo cast, 135
Bomber Long "A", 133
Bomber Magnum Long "A", 127
Boogerman Muskie Buzz, 122
Botsford, Harry, 26
Bottom fishing, 109–110
Braided-wire leader, 61
Bucher Baby Shallow Raider, 94
Bucher Baby Tail, 127
Bucher Depth Raider, 127
Bucher Jointed Shallow Raider, 127
Buchertail, 122
Bucher Tandem Buzzer, 139
Bucktail jig with conehead, 86
Bucktails, 80–81
    jigs and, 85
    for night fishing, 144
    size of, 80
    spinner, 74
    spinnerbaits, 82
    for spring-hole fishing, 139
    tips for fishing with, 81
    types of, 81

    for weedy-cover fishing, 122
Bull Dawg, 97
Bulrushes, 121
Butt seats, 64
Buzzbaits
    getaway technique, 91
    for spring-hole fishing, 139

C

Cabbage, 120
Casting, 113, 115
    bolo cast, 135
    fishing tips for, 115
    pitchin' technique, 135
Casting spoons, 101
Catch-and-release, 30–31
    hooks and, 31
    letting fish go, 30–31
    nets and, 31
    in oligotrophic lakes, 41
Chain pickerel
    physical characteristics of, 15
    range of, 15
    world record of, 15
Chubs, 107
    for ice fishing, 148
Ciscoes, 16, 18, 46, 75, 107
    for ice fishing, 148, 151
    in mesotrophic lakes, 38
    in oligotrophic lakes, 40
Cisco Kid, 94, 122
Cisco Kid Topper, 90
Clarity of water, 16
    crawlers and, 89
    in deep reservoirs, 46
    in eutrophic lakes, 37
    habitat for pike and muskies and,
        35
    in mesotrophic lakes, 38
    night fishing and, 143
    in shallow reservoirs, 42–43
    spooking and, 127
    stickbaits and, 89
Clear muskie, 14
Cold fronts, 130–131
    pike and muskies' reaction to,
        130
    rivers and, 131
    spinnerbaits and, 131
    tips for fishing in, 130–131
Color phases
    of muskie, 12, 14
Color preference

    jigs and, 85
    lures and, 79
    muskie and, 75, 85
    night fishing and, 144
    pike and, 75, 85
Conservation of pike/muskies, 28–29
Coontail, 120
Crankbait, 93, 127
    for night fishing, 144
    for spring-hole fishing, 141
    for weedy-cover fishing, 122
Crawlers, 89
Crayfish, fly, 105
Current
    habitat for pike and muskies and,
        35

D

Dacron, 59
Dardevle, 127
Dardevle 5-Diamonds, 102
Darkhouse spearing, 29
Deep reservoirs, 46–47
Deep trolling, 154
Depth finder, 66–67
    characteristics of good, 67
Depth-Therm, 138
Divers, jerkbait, 97
    tips on working, 98
Doctor Spoon, 102
Downrigger fishing
    tackle for, 127
    trolling, 126–128
Drifter Believer, 122
Drifter Jointed Believer, 127
Drifting, 112–113
    fishing tips for, 115

E

Economy tip-ups, 149
Electric thermometer, 138
End plate, 68
Esocids, 8
Eurasian pike, 9
Eurasian water milfoil, 121
Eutrophic lakes, 36–37

F

Feeding habits, 16–17
    of muskie, 9, 12
    of pike, 9
    water temperature and, 16
Figure-8 technique, 76, 77